THIS BOOK BELONGS TO

CONTACT INFORMATION	
NAME	
PHONE #	
ADDRESS	
EMAIL	

Copyright © Teresa Rother
All rights reserved. No part of this publication may be reproduced, distributed, or transmitted in any form or by any means, including photocopy, recording, or other electronic or mechanical methods.

DEDICATION

This Wine Tasting Journal is dedicated to wine lovers who want to document their wine tasting experience.

You are my inspiration for producing this book and I'm honored to be a part of capturing the special moments of tasting, reviewing, and recording your journey.

HOW TO USE THIS BOOK

This Wine Tasting Journal will allow you to accurately record every detail of your personal experience as you savor the appearance, aromas, taste of wine varieties. It's a great way to document names, vintage, region, hues, intensity, and much more.

Here are examples of information for you to fill in and write the details about your experience in this book.

Fill in the following information:

1. Wine Information - Name, origin, type, vintage, orchard region, varietal, and alcohol percentage.
2. Hues - Record wine appearance.
3. Intensity - Record intensity for red, rose, and white.
4. Aroma - Record the wine's fragrance and blank spaces for secondary notes.
5. Taste - Record wine flavors using the different categories.
6. Rate - On a scale of 1 to 10 rate sweetness, acidity, tannins, body, flavor intensity, and finish.
7. Pairs Well With - A place to write down food and snacks that pair well with the wine.
8. Review Notes - Space to write additional information.
9. Would You Buy Again? - Yes or No
10. Overall Rating - Rate the wine on a scale of 1 to 10.

WINE TASTING

NAME		ORCHARD	
ORIGIN		REGION	
TYPE		VARIETAL	
VINTAGE		ALCOHOL %	

HUES		
○ STRAW	○ YELLOW	○ GOLD
○ BROWN	○ AMBER	○ COPPER
○ SALMON	○ PINK	○ RUBY
○ PURPLE	○ GARNET	○ TAWNY

INTENSITY		
RED	ROSÉ	WHITE
○ PALE	○ PALE	○ PALE
○ MEDIUM	○ MEDIUM	○ MEDIUM
○ DEEP	○ DEEP	○ DEEP

AROMA		
○ FRUIT	○ FLORAL	○ HERBAL
○ YEAST	○ SPICE	○ NUT
○ EARTH	○ OAK	○ VEGETAL
○	○	○

TASTE		
○ CITRUS	○ BERRIES	○ COFFEE
○ MINERAL	○ SPICE	○ NUT
○ EARTH	○ BARREL	○ VANILLA
○ COCOA	○	○

SWEETNESS	ACIDITY	TANNINS
1 2 3 4 5 6 7 8 9 10	1 2 3 4 5 6 7 8 9 10	1 2 3 4 5 6 7 8 9 10

BODY	FLAVOR INTENSITY	FINISH
1 2 3 4 5 6 7 8 9 10	1 2 3 4 5 6 7 8 9 10	1 2 3 4 5 6 7 8 9 10

PAIRS WELL WITH	REVIEW NOTES

WOULD YOU BUY IT AGAIN?		OVERALL RATING
○ YES	○ NO	/10

WINE TASTING

NAME		ORCHARD	
ORIGIN		REGION	
TYPE		VARIETAL	
VINTAGE		ALCOHOL %	

HUES

○ STRAW	○ YELLOW	○ GOLD
○ BROWN	○ AMBER	○ COPPER
○ SALMON	○ PINK	○ RUBY
○ PURPLE	○ GARNET	○ TAWNY

INTENSITY

RED	ROSÉ	WHITE
○ PALE	○ PALE	○ PALE
○ MEDIUM	○ MEDIUM	○ MEDIUM
○ DEEP	○ DEEP	○ DEEP

AROMA

○ FRUIT	○ FLORAL	○ HERBAL
○ YEAST	○ SPICE	○ NUT
○ EARTH	○ OAK	○ VEGETAL
○	○	○

TASTE

○ CITRUS	○ BERRIES	○ COFFEE
○ MINERAL	○ SPICE	○ NUT
○ EARTH	○ BARREL	○ VANILLA
○ COCOA	○	○

SWEETNESS	ACIDITY	TANNINS
1 2 3 4 5 6 7 8 9 10	1 2 3 4 5 6 7 8 9 10	1 2 3 4 5 6 7 8 9 10

BODY	FLAVOR INTENSITY	FINISH
1 2 3 4 5 6 7 8 9 10	1 2 3 4 5 6 7 8 9 10	1 2 3 4 5 6 7 8 9 10

PAIRS WELL WITH	REVIEW NOTES

WOULD YOU BUY IT AGAIN?		OVERALL RATING
○ YES	○ NO	/10

WINE TASTING

NAME		ORCHARD	
ORIGIN		REGION	
TYPE		VARIETAL	
VINTAGE		ALCOHOL %	

HUES			INTENSITY		
			RED	ROSÉ	WHITE
○ STRAW	○ YELLOW	○ GOLD	○ PALE	○ PALE	○ PALE
○ BROWN	○ AMBER	○ COPPER	○ MEDIUM	○ MEDIUM	○ MEDIUM
○ SALMON	○ PINK	○ RUBY	○ DEEP	○ DEEP	○ DEEP
○ PURPLE	○ GARNET	○ TAWNY			

AROMA			TASTE		
○ FRUIT	○ FLORAL	○ HERBAL	○ CITRUS	○ BERRIES	○ COFFEE
○ YEAST	○ SPICE	○ NUT	○ MINERAL	○ SPICE	○ NUT
○ EARTH	○ OAK	○ VEGETAL	○ EARTH	○ BARREL	○ VANILLA
○	○	○	○ COCOA	○	○

SWEETNESS	ACIDITY	TANNINS
1 2 3 4 5 6 7 8 9 10	1 2 3 4 5 6 7 8 9 10	1 2 3 4 5 6 7 8 9 10

BODY	FLAVOR INTENSITY	FINISH
1 2 3 4 5 6 7 8 9 10	1 2 3 4 5 6 7 8 9 10	1 2 3 4 5 6 7 8 9 10

PAIRS WELL WITH	REVIEW NOTES

WOULD YOU BUY IT AGAIN?		OVERALL RATING
○ YES	○ NO	/10

WINE TASTING

NAME		ORCHARD	
ORIGIN		REGION	
TYPE		VARIETAL	
VINTAGE		ALCOHOL %	

HUES		
○ STRAW	○ YELLOW	○ GOLD
○ BROWN	○ AMBER	○ COPPER
○ SALMON	○ PINK	○ RUBY
○ PURPLE	○ GARNET	○ TAWNY

INTENSITY		
RED	ROSÉ	WHITE
○ PALE	○ PALE	○ PALE
○ MEDIUM	○ MEDIUM	○ MEDIUM
○ DEEP	○ DEEP	○ DEEP

AROMA		
○ FRUIT	○ FLORAL	○ HERBAL
○ YEAST	○ SPICE	○ NUT
○ EARTH	○ OAK	○ VEGETAL
○	○	○

TASTE		
○ CITRUS	○ BERRIES	○ COFFEE
○ MINERAL	○ SPICE	○ NUT
○ EARTH	○ BARREL	○ VANILLA
○ COCOA	○	○

SWEETNESS	ACIDITY	TANNINS
1 2 3 4 5 6 7 8 9 10	1 2 3 4 5 6 7 8 9 10	1 2 3 4 5 6 7 8 9 10

BODY	FLAVOR INTENSITY	FINISH
1 2 3 4 5 6 7 8 9 10	1 2 3 4 5 6 7 8 9 10	1 2 3 4 5 6 7 8 9 10

PAIRS WELL WITH	REVIEW NOTES

WOULD YOU BUY IT AGAIN?		OVERALL RATING
○ YES	○ NO	/10

WINE TASTING

NAME		ORCHARD	
ORIGIN		REGION	
TYPE		VARIETAL	
VINTAGE		ALCOHOL %	

HUES		
○ STRAW	○ YELLOW	○ GOLD
○ BROWN	○ AMBER	○ COPPER
○ SALMON	○ PINK	○ RUBY
○ PURPLE	○ GARNET	○ TAWNY

INTENSITY		
RED	ROSÉ	WHITE
○ PALE	○ PALE	○ PALE
○ MEDIUM	○ MEDIUM	○ MEDIUM
○ DEEP	○ DEEP	○ DEEP

AROMA		
○ FRUIT	○ FLORAL	○ HERBAL
○ YEAST	○ SPICE	○ NUT
○ EARTH	○ OAK	○ VEGETAL
○	○	○

TASTE		
○ CITRUS	○ BERRIES	○ COFFEE
○ MINERAL	○ SPICE	○ NUT
○ EARTH	○ BARREL	○ VANILLA
○ COCOA	○	○

SWEETNESS	ACIDITY	TANNINS
1 2 3 4 5 6 7 8 9 10	1 2 3 4 5 6 7 8 9 10	1 2 3 4 5 6 7 8 9 10

BODY	FLAVOR INTENSITY	FINISH
1 2 3 4 5 6 7 8 9 10	1 2 3 4 5 6 7 8 9 10	1 2 3 4 5 6 7 8 9 10

PAIRS WELL WITH	REVIEW NOTES

WOULD YOU BUY IT AGAIN?		OVERALL RATING
○ YES	○ NO	/10

WINE TASTING

NAME		ORCHARD	
ORIGIN		REGION	
TYPE		VARIETAL	
VINTAGE		ALCOHOL %	

HUES			INTENSITY		
			RED	ROSÉ	WHITE
○ STRAW	○ YELLOW	○ GOLD	○ PALE	○ PALE	○ PALE
○ BROWN	○ AMBER	○ COPPER	○ MEDIUM	○ MEDIUM	○ MEDIUM
○ SALMON	○ PINK	○ RUBY	○ DEEP	○ DEEP	○ DEEP
○ PURPLE	○ GARNET	○ TAWNY			

AROMA			TASTE		
○ FRUIT	○ FLORAL	○ HERBAL	○ CITRUS	○ BERRIES	○ COFFEE
○ YEAST	○ SPICE	○ NUT	○ MINERAL	○ SPICE	○ NUT
○ EARTH	○ OAK	○ VEGETAL	○ EARTH	○ BARREL	○ VANILLA
○	○	○	○ COCOA	○	○

SWEETNESS	ACIDITY	TANNINS
1 2 3 4 5 6 7 8 9 10	1 2 3 4 5 6 7 8 9 10	1 2 3 4 5 6 7 8 9 10

BODY	FLAVOR INTENSITY	FINISH
1 2 3 4 5 6 7 8 9 10	1 2 3 4 5 6 7 8 9 10	1 2 3 4 5 6 7 8 9 10

PAIRS WELL WITH	REVIEW NOTES

WOULD YOU BUY IT AGAIN?		OVERALL RATING
○ YES	○ NO	/10

WINE TASTING

NAME		ORCHARD	
ORIGIN		REGION	
TYPE		VARIETAL	
VINTAGE		ALCOHOL %	

HUES			INTENSITY		
○ STRAW	○ YELLOW	○ GOLD	RED	ROSÉ	WHITE
○ BROWN	○ AMBER	○ COPPER	○ PALE	○ PALE	○ PALE
○ SALMON	○ PINK	○ RUBY	○ MEDIUM	○ MEDIUM	○ MEDIUM
○ PURPLE	○ GARNET	○ TAWNY	○ DEEP	○ DEEP	○ DEEP

AROMA			TASTE		
○ FRUIT	○ FLORAL	○ HERBAL	○ CITRUS	○ BERRIES	○ COFFEE
○ YEAST	○ SPICE	○ NUT	○ MINERAL	○ SPICE	○ NUT
○ EARTH	○ OAK	○ VEGETAL	○ EARTH	○ BARREL	○ VANILLA
○	○	○	○ COCOA	○	○

SWEETNESS	ACIDITY	TANNINS
1 2 3 4 5 6 7 8 9 10	1 2 3 4 5 6 7 8 9 10	1 2 3 4 5 6 7 8 9 10

BODY	FLAVOR INTENSITY	FINISH
1 2 3 4 5 6 7 8 9 10	1 2 3 4 5 6 7 8 9 10	1 2 3 4 5 6 7 8 9 10

PAIRS WELL WITH	REVIEW NOTES

WOULD YOU BUY IT AGAIN?		OVERALL RATING
○ YES	○ NO	/10

WINE TASTING

NAME		ORCHARD	
ORIGIN		REGION	
TYPE		VARIETAL	
VINTAGE		ALCOHOL %	

HUES			INTENSITY		
			RED	ROSÉ	WHITE
○ STRAW	○ YELLOW	○ GOLD			
○ BROWN	○ AMBER	○ COPPER	○ PALE	○ PALE	○ PALE
○ SALMON	○ PINK	○ RUBY	○ MEDIUM	○ MEDIUM	○ MEDIUM
○ PURPLE	○ GARNET	○ TAWNY	○ DEEP	○ DEEP	○ DEEP

AROMA			TASTE		
○ FRUIT	○ FLORAL	○ HERBAL	○ CITRUS	○ BERRIES	○ COFFEE
○ YEAST	○ SPICE	○ NUT	○ MINERAL	○ SPICE	○ NUT
○ EARTH	○ OAK	○ VEGETAL	○ EARTH	○ BARREL	○ VANILLA
○	○	○	○ COCOA	○	○

SWEETNESS	ACIDITY	TANNINS
1 2 3 4 5 6 7 8 9 10	1 2 3 4 5 6 7 8 9 10	1 2 3 4 5 6 7 8 9 10

BODY	FLAVOR INTENSITY	FINISH
1 2 3 4 5 6 7 8 9 10	1 2 3 4 5 6 7 8 9 10	1 2 3 4 5 6 7 8 9 10

PAIRS WELL WITH	REVIEW NOTES

WOULD YOU BUY IT AGAIN?		OVERALL RATING
○ YES	○ NO	/10

WINE TASTING

NAME		ORCHARD	
ORIGIN		REGION	
TYPE		VARIETAL	
VINTAGE		ALCOHOL %	

HUES			INTENSITY		
			RED	ROSÉ	WHITE
○ STRAW	○ YELLOW	○ GOLD	○ PALE	○ PALE	○ PALE
○ BROWN	○ AMBER	○ COPPER	○ MEDIUM	○ MEDIUM	○ MEDIUM
○ SALMON	○ PINK	○ RUBY	○ DEEP	○ DEEP	○ DEEP
○ PURPLE	○ GARNET	○ TAWNY			

AROMA			TASTE		
○ FRUIT	○ FLORAL	○ HERBAL	○ CITRUS	○ BERRIES	○ COFFEE
○ YEAST	○ SPICE	○ NUT	○ MINERAL	○ SPICE	○ NUT
○ EARTH	○ OAK	○ VEGETAL	○ EARTH	○ BARREL	○ VANILLA
○	○	○	○ COCOA	○	○

SWEETNESS	ACIDITY	TANNINS
1 2 3 4 5 6 7 8 9 10	1 2 3 4 5 6 7 8 9 10	1 2 3 4 5 6 7 8 9 10

BODY	FLAVOR INTENSITY	FINISH
1 2 3 4 5 6 7 8 9 10	1 2 3 4 5 6 7 8 9 10	1 2 3 4 5 6 7 8 9 10

PAIRS WELL WITH	REVIEW NOTES

WOULD YOU BUY IT AGAIN?		OVERALL RATING
○ YES	○ NO	/10

WINE TASTING

NAME		ORCHARD	
ORIGIN		REGION	
TYPE		VARIETAL	
VINTAGE		ALCOHOL %	

HUES			INTENSITY		
			RED	ROSÉ	WHITE
○ STRAW	○ YELLOW	○ GOLD	○ PALE	○ PALE	○ PALE
○ BROWN	○ AMBER	○ COPPER	○ MEDIUM	○ MEDIUM	○ MEDIUM
○ SALMON	○ PINK	○ RUBY	○ DEEP	○ DEEP	○ DEEP
○ PURPLE	○ GARNET	○ TAWNY			

AROMA			TASTE		
○ FRUIT	○ FLORAL	○ HERBAL	○ CITRUS	○ BERRIES	○ COFFEE
○ YEAST	○ SPICE	○ NUT	○ MINERAL	○ SPICE	○ NUT
○ EARTH	○ OAK	○ VEGETAL	○ EARTH	○ BARREL	○ VANILLA
○	○	○	○ COCOA	○	○

SWEETNESS	ACIDITY	TANNINS
1 2 3 4 5 6 7 8 9 10	1 2 3 4 5 6 7 8 9 10	1 2 3 4 5 6 7 8 9 10

BODY	FLAVOR INTENSITY	FINISH
1 2 3 4 5 6 7 8 9 10	1 2 3 4 5 6 7 8 9 10	1 2 3 4 5 6 7 8 9 10

PAIRS WELL WITH	REVIEW NOTES

WOULD YOU BUY IT AGAIN?		OVERALL RATING
○ YES	○ NO	/10

WINE TASTING

NAME		ORCHARD	
ORIGIN		REGION	
TYPE		VARIETAL	
VINTAGE		ALCOHOL %	

HUES			INTENSITY		
○ STRAW	○ YELLOW	○ GOLD	RED	ROSÉ	WHITE
○ BROWN	○ AMBER	○ COPPER	○ PALE	○ PALE	○ PALE
○ SALMON	○ PINK	○ RUBY	○ MEDIUM	○ MEDIUM	○ MEDIUM
○ PURPLE	○ GARNET	○ TAWNY	○ DEEP	○ DEEP	○ DEEP

AROMA			TASTE		
○ FRUIT	○ FLORAL	○ HERBAL	○ CITRUS	○ BERRIES	○ COFFEE
○ YEAST	○ SPICE	○ NUT	○ MINERAL	○ SPICE	○ NUT
○ EARTH	○ OAK	○ VEGETAL	○ EARTH	○ BARREL	○ VANILLA
○	○	○	○ COCOA	○	○

SWEETNESS	ACIDITY	TANNINS
1 2 3 4 5 6 7 8 9 10	1 2 3 4 5 6 7 8 9 10	1 2 3 4 5 6 7 8 9 10

BODY	FLAVOR INTENSITY	FINISH
1 2 3 4 5 6 7 8 9 10	1 2 3 4 5 6 7 8 9 10	1 2 3 4 5 6 7 8 9 10

PAIRS WELL WITH	REVIEW NOTES

WOULD YOU BUY IT AGAIN?		OVERALL RATING
○ YES	○ NO	/10

WINE TASTING

NAME		ORCHARD	
ORIGIN		REGION	
TYPE		VARIETAL	
VINTAGE		ALCOHOL %	

HUES			INTENSITY		
			RED	ROSÉ	WHITE
○ STRAW	○ YELLOW	○ GOLD			
○ BROWN	○ AMBER	○ COPPER	○ PALE	○ PALE	○ PALE
○ SALMON	○ PINK	○ RUBY	○ MEDIUM	○ MEDIUM	○ MEDIUM
○ PURPLE	○ GARNET	○ TAWNY	○ DEEP	○ DEEP	○ DEEP

AROMA			TASTE		
○ FRUIT	○ FLORAL	○ HERBAL	○ CITRUS	○ BERRIES	○ COFFEE
○ YEAST	○ SPICE	○ NUT	○ MINERAL	○ SPICE	○ NUT
○ EARTH	○ OAK	○ VEGETAL	○ EARTH	○ BARREL	○ VANILLA
○	○	○	○ COCOA	○	○

SWEETNESS	ACIDITY	TANNINS
1 2 3 4 5 6 7 8 9 10	1 2 3 4 5 6 7 8 9 10	1 2 3 4 5 6 7 8 9 10

BODY	FLAVOR INTENSITY	FINISH
1 2 3 4 5 6 7 8 9 10	1 2 3 4 5 6 7 8 9 10	1 2 3 4 5 6 7 8 9 10

PAIRS WELL WITH	REVIEW NOTES

WOULD YOU BUY IT AGAIN?		OVERALL RATING
○ YES	○ NO	/10

WINE TASTING

NAME		ORCHARD	
ORIGIN		REGION	
TYPE		VARIETAL	
VINTAGE		ALCOHOL %	

HUES			INTENSITY		
○ STRAW	○ YELLOW	○ GOLD	RED	ROSÉ	WHITE
○ BROWN	○ AMBER	○ COPPER	○ PALE	○ PALE	○ PALE
○ SALMON	○ PINK	○ RUBY	○ MEDIUM	○ MEDIUM	○ MEDIUM
○ PURPLE	○ GARNET	○ TAWNY	○ DEEP	○ DEEP	○ DEEP

AROMA			TASTE		
○ FRUIT	○ FLORAL	○ HERBAL	○ CITRUS	○ BERRIES	○ COFFEE
○ YEAST	○ SPICE	○ NUT	○ MINERAL	○ SPICE	○ NUT
○ EARTH	○ OAK	○ VEGETAL	○ EARTH	○ BARREL	○ VANILLA
○	○	○	○ COCOA	○	○

SWEETNESS	ACIDITY	TANNINS
1 2 3 4 5 6 7 8 9 10	1 2 3 4 5 6 7 8 9 10	1 2 3 4 5 6 7 8 9 10

BODY	FLAVOR INTENSITY	FINISH
1 2 3 4 5 6 7 8 9 10	1 2 3 4 5 6 7 8 9 10	1 2 3 4 5 6 7 8 9 10

PAIRS WELL WITH	REVIEW NOTES

WOULD YOU BUY IT AGAIN?		OVERALL RATING
○ YES	○ NO	/10

WINE TASTING

NAME		ORCHARD	
ORIGIN		REGION	
TYPE		VARIETAL	
VINTAGE		ALCOHOL %	

HUES

○ STRAW	○ YELLOW	○ GOLD
○ BROWN	○ AMBER	○ COPPER
○ SALMON	○ PINK	○ RUBY
○ PURPLE	○ GARNET	○ TAWNY

INTENSITY

RED	ROSÉ	WHITE
○ PALE	○ PALE	○ PALE
○ MEDIUM	○ MEDIUM	○ MEDIUM
○ DEEP	○ DEEP	○ DEEP

AROMA

○ FRUIT	○ FLORAL	○ HERBAL
○ YEAST	○ SPICE	○ NUT
○ EARTH	○ OAK	○ VEGETAL
○	○	○

TASTE

○ CITRUS	○ BERRIES	○ COFFEE
○ MINERAL	○ SPICE	○ NUT
○ EARTH	○ BARREL	○ VANILLA
○ COCOA	○	○

SWEETNESS	ACIDITY	TANNINS
1 2 3 4 5 6 7 8 9 10	1 2 3 4 5 6 7 8 9 10	1 2 3 4 5 6 7 8 9 10

BODY	FLAVOR INTENSITY	FINISH
1 2 3 4 5 6 7 8 9 10	1 2 3 4 5 6 7 8 9 10	1 2 3 4 5 6 7 8 9 10

PAIRS WELL WITH	REVIEW NOTES

WOULD YOU BUY IT AGAIN?		OVERALL RATING
○ YES	○ NO	/10

WINE TASTING

NAME		ORCHARD	
ORIGIN		REGION	
TYPE		VARIETAL	
VINTAGE		ALCOHOL %	

HUES			INTENSITY		
			RED	ROSÉ	WHITE
○ STRAW	○ YELLOW	○ GOLD	○ PALE	○ PALE	○ PALE
○ BROWN	○ AMBER	○ COPPER	○ MEDIUM	○ MEDIUM	○ MEDIUM
○ SALMON	○ PINK	○ RUBY	○ DEEP	○ DEEP	○ DEEP
○ PURPLE	○ GARNET	○ TAWNY			

AROMA			TASTE		
○ FRUIT	○ FLORAL	○ HERBAL	○ CITRUS	○ BERRIES	○ COFFEE
○ YEAST	○ SPICE	○ NUT	○ MINERAL	○ SPICE	○ NUT
○ EARTH	○ OAK	○ VEGETAL	○ EARTH	○ BARREL	○ VANILLA
○	○	○	○ COCOA	○	○

SWEETNESS	ACIDITY	TANNINS
1 2 3 4 5 6 7 8 9 10	1 2 3 4 5 6 7 8 9 10	1 2 3 4 5 6 7 8 9 10

BODY	FLAVOR INTENSITY	FINISH
1 2 3 4 5 6 7 8 9 10	1 2 3 4 5 6 7 8 9 10	1 2 3 4 5 6 7 8 9 10

PAIRS WELL WITH	REVIEW NOTES

WOULD YOU BUY IT AGAIN?		OVERALL RATING
○ YES	○ NO	/10

WINE TASTING

NAME		ORCHARD	
ORIGIN		REGION	
TYPE		VARIETAL	
VINTAGE		ALCOHOL %	

HUES			INTENSITY		
○ STRAW	○ YELLOW	○ GOLD	RED	ROSÉ	WHITE
○ BROWN	○ AMBER	○ COPPER	○ PALE	○ PALE	○ PALE
○ SALMON	○ PINK	○ RUBY	○ MEDIUM	○ MEDIUM	○ MEDIUM
○ PURPLE	○ GARNET	○ TAWNY	○ DEEP	○ DEEP	○ DEEP

AROMA			TASTE		
○ FRUIT	○ FLORAL	○ HERBAL	○ CITRUS	○ BERRIES	○ COFFEE
○ YEAST	○ SPICE	○ NUT	○ MINERAL	○ SPICE	○ NUT
○ EARTH	○ OAK	○ VEGETAL	○ EARTH	○ BARREL	○ VANILLA
○	○	○	○ COCOA	○	○

SWEETNESS	ACIDITY	TANNINS
1 2 3 4 5 6 7 8 9 10	1 2 3 4 5 6 7 8 9 10	1 2 3 4 5 6 7 8 9 10

BODY	FLAVOR INTENSITY	FINISH
1 2 3 4 5 6 7 8 9 10	1 2 3 4 5 6 7 8 9 10	1 2 3 4 5 6 7 8 9 10

PAIRS WELL WITH	REVIEW NOTES

WOULD YOU BUY IT AGAIN?		OVERALL RATING
○ YES	○ NO	/10

WINE TASTING

NAME		ORCHARD	
ORIGIN		REGION	
TYPE		VARIETAL	
VINTAGE		ALCOHOL %	

HUES			INTENSITY		
○ STRAW	○ YELLOW	○ GOLD	RED	ROSÉ	WHITE
○ BROWN	○ AMBER	○ COPPER	○ PALE	○ PALE	○ PALE
○ SALMON	○ PINK	○ RUBY	○ MEDIUM	○ MEDIUM	○ MEDIUM
○ PURPLE	○ GARNET	○ TAWNY	○ DEEP	○ DEEP	○ DEEP

AROMA			TASTE		
○ FRUIT	○ FLORAL	○ HERBAL	○ CITRUS	○ BERRIES	○ COFFEE
○ YEAST	○ SPICE	○ NUT	○ MINERAL	○ SPICE	○ NUT
○ EARTH	○ OAK	○ VEGETAL	○ EARTH	○ BARREL	○ VANILLA
○	○	○	○ COCOA	○	○

SWEETNESS	ACIDITY	TANNINS
1 2 3 4 5 6 7 8 9 10	1 2 3 4 5 6 7 8 9 10	1 2 3 4 5 6 7 8 9 10

BODY	FLAVOR INTENSITY	FINISH
1 2 3 4 5 6 7 8 9 10	1 2 3 4 5 6 7 8 9 10	1 2 3 4 5 6 7 8 9 10

PAIRS WELL WITH	REVIEW NOTES

WOULD YOU BUY IT AGAIN?		OVERALL RATING
○ YES	○ NO	/10

WINE TASTING

NAME		ORCHARD	
ORIGIN		REGION	
TYPE		VARIETAL	
VINTAGE		ALCOHOL %	

HUES			INTENSITY		
○ STRAW	○ YELLOW	○ GOLD	RED	ROSÉ	WHITE
○ BROWN	○ AMBER	○ COPPER	○ PALE	○ PALE	○ PALE
○ SALMON	○ PINK	○ RUBY	○ MEDIUM	○ MEDIUM	○ MEDIUM
○ PURPLE	○ GARNET	○ TAWNY	○ DEEP	○ DEEP	○ DEEP

AROMA			TASTE		
○ FRUIT	○ FLORAL	○ HERBAL	○ CITRUS	○ BERRIES	○ COFFEE
○ YEAST	○ SPICE	○ NUT	○ MINERAL	○ SPICE	○ NUT
○ EARTH	○ OAK	○ VEGETAL	○ EARTH	○ BARREL	○ VANILLA
○	○	○	○ COCOA	○	○

SWEETNESS	ACIDITY	TANNINS
1 2 3 4 5 6 7 8 9 10	1 2 3 4 5 6 7 8 9 10	1 2 3 4 5 6 7 8 9 10

BODY	FLAVOR INTENSITY	FINISH
1 2 3 4 5 6 7 8 9 10	1 2 3 4 5 6 7 8 9 10	1 2 3 4 5 6 7 8 9 10

PAIRS WELL WITH	REVIEW NOTES

WOULD YOU BUY IT AGAIN?		OVERALL RATING
○ YES	○ NO	/10

WINE TASTING

NAME		ORCHARD	
ORIGIN		REGION	
TYPE		VARIETAL	
VINTAGE		ALCOHOL %	

HUES		
○ STRAW	○ YELLOW	○ GOLD
○ BROWN	○ AMBER	○ COPPER
○ SALMON	○ PINK	○ RUBY
○ PURPLE	○ GARNET	○ TAWNY

INTENSITY		
RED	ROSÉ	WHITE
○ PALE	○ PALE	○ PALE
○ MEDIUM	○ MEDIUM	○ MEDIUM
○ DEEP	○ DEEP	○ DEEP

AROMA		
○ FRUIT	○ FLORAL	○ HERBAL
○ YEAST	○ SPICE	○ NUT
○ EARTH	○ OAK	○ VEGETAL
○	○	○

TASTE		
○ CITRUS	○ BERRIES	○ COFFEE
○ MINERAL	○ SPICE	○ NUT
○ EARTH	○ BARREL	○ VANILLA
○ COCOA	○	○

SWEETNESS	ACIDITY	TANNINS
1 2 3 4 5 6 7 8 9 10	1 2 3 4 5 6 7 8 9 10	1 2 3 4 5 6 7 8 9 10

BODY	FLAVOR INTENSITY	FINISH
1 2 3 4 5 6 7 8 9 10	1 2 3 4 5 6 7 8 9 10	1 2 3 4 5 6 7 8 9 10

PAIRS WELL WITH	REVIEW NOTES

WOULD YOU BUY IT AGAIN?		OVERALL RATING
○ YES	○ NO	/10

WINE TASTING

NAME		ORCHARD	
ORIGIN		REGION	
TYPE		VARIETAL	
VINTAGE		ALCOHOL %	

HUES			INTENSITY		
○ STRAW	○ YELLOW	○ GOLD	RED	ROSÉ	WHITE
○ BROWN	○ AMBER	○ COPPER	○ PALE	○ PALE	○ PALE
○ SALMON	○ PINK	○ RUBY	○ MEDIUM	○ MEDIUM	○ MEDIUM
○ PURPLE	○ GARNET	○ TAWNY	○ DEEP	○ DEEP	○ DEEP

AROMA			TASTE		
○ FRUIT	○ FLORAL	○ HERBAL	○ CITRUS	○ BERRIES	○ COFFEE
○ YEAST	○ SPICE	○ NUT	○ MINERAL	○ SPICE	○ NUT
○ EARTH	○ OAK	○ VEGETAL	○ EARTH	○ BARREL	○ VANILLA
○	○	○	○ COCOA	○	○

SWEETNESS	ACIDITY	TANNINS
1 2 3 4 5 6 7 8 9 10	1 2 3 4 5 6 7 8 9 10	1 2 3 4 5 6 7 8 9 10

BODY	FLAVOR INTENSITY	FINISH
1 2 3 4 5 6 7 8 9 10	1 2 3 4 5 6 7 8 9 10	1 2 3 4 5 6 7 8 9 10

PAIRS WELL WITH	REVIEW NOTES

WOULD YOU BUY IT AGAIN?		OVERALL RATING
○ YES	○ NO	/10

WINE TASTING

NAME		ORCHARD	
ORIGIN		REGION	
TYPE		VARIETAL	
VINTAGE		ALCOHOL %	

HUES			INTENSITY		
			RED	ROSÉ	WHITE
○ STRAW	○ YELLOW	○ GOLD	○ PALE	○ PALE	○ PALE
○ BROWN	○ AMBER	○ COPPER	○ MEDIUM	○ MEDIUM	○ MEDIUM
○ SALMON	○ PINK	○ RUBY	○ DEEP	○ DEEP	○ DEEP
○ PURPLE	○ GARNET	○ TAWNY			

AROMA			TASTE		
○ FRUIT	○ FLORAL	○ HERBAL	○ CITRUS	○ BERRIES	○ COFFEE
○ YEAST	○ SPICE	○ NUT	○ MINERAL	○ SPICE	○ NUT
○ EARTH	○ OAK	○ VEGETAL	○ EARTH	○ BARREL	○ VANILLA
○	○	○	○ COCOA	○	○

SWEETNESS	ACIDITY	TANNINS
1 2 3 4 5 6 7 8 9 10	1 2 3 4 5 6 7 8 9 10	1 2 3 4 5 6 7 8 9 10

BODY	FLAVOR INTENSITY	FINISH
1 2 3 4 5 6 7 8 9 10	1 2 3 4 5 6 7 8 9 10	1 2 3 4 5 6 7 8 9 10

PAIRS WELL WITH	REVIEW NOTES

WOULD YOU BUY IT AGAIN?		OVERALL RATING
○ YES	○ NO	/10

WINE TASTING

NAME		ORCHARD	
ORIGIN		REGION	
TYPE		VARIETAL	
VINTAGE		ALCOHOL %	

HUES			INTENSITY		
			RED	ROSÉ	WHITE
○ STRAW	○ YELLOW	○ GOLD			
○ BROWN	○ AMBER	○ COPPER	○ PALE	○ PALE	○ PALE
○ SALMON	○ PINK	○ RUBY	○ MEDIUM	○ MEDIUM	○ MEDIUM
○ PURPLE	○ GARNET	○ TAWNY	○ DEEP	○ DEEP	○ DEEP

AROMA			TASTE		
○ FRUIT	○ FLORAL	○ HERBAL	○ CITRUS	○ BERRIES	○ COFFEE
○ YEAST	○ SPICE	○ NUT	○ MINERAL	○ SPICE	○ NUT
○ EARTH	○ OAK	○ VEGETAL	○ EARTH	○ BARREL	○ VANILLA
○	○	○	○ COCOA	○	○

SWEETNESS	ACIDITY	TANNINS
1 2 3 4 5 6 7 8 9 10	1 2 3 4 5 6 7 8 9 10	1 2 3 4 5 6 7 8 9 10

BODY	FLAVOR INTENSITY	FINISH
1 2 3 4 5 6 7 8 9 10	1 2 3 4 5 6 7 8 9 10	1 2 3 4 5 6 7 8 9 10

PAIRS WELL WITH	REVIEW NOTES

WOULD YOU BUY IT AGAIN?		OVERALL RATING
○ YES	○ NO	/10

WINE TASTING

NAME		ORCHARD	
ORIGIN		REGION	
TYPE		VARIETAL	
VINTAGE		ALCOHOL %	

HUES			INTENSITY		
			RED	ROSÉ	WHITE
○ STRAW	○ YELLOW	○ GOLD	○ PALE	○ PALE	○ PALE
○ BROWN	○ AMBER	○ COPPER	○ MEDIUM	○ MEDIUM	○ MEDIUM
○ SALMON	○ PINK	○ RUBY	○ DEEP	○ DEEP	○ DEEP
○ PURPLE	○ GARNET	○ TAWNY			

AROMA			TASTE		
○ FRUIT	○ FLORAL	○ HERBAL	○ CITRUS	○ BERRIES	○ COFFEE
○ YEAST	○ SPICE	○ NUT	○ MINERAL	○ SPICE	○ NUT
○ EARTH	○ OAK	○ VEGETAL	○ EARTH	○ BARREL	○ VANILLA
○	○	○	○ COCOA	○	○

SWEETNESS	ACIDITY	TANNINS
1 2 3 4 5 6 7 8 9 10	1 2 3 4 5 6 7 8 9 10	1 2 3 4 5 6 7 8 9 10

BODY	FLAVOR INTENSITY	FINISH
1 2 3 4 5 6 7 8 9 10	1 2 3 4 5 6 7 8 9 10	1 2 3 4 5 6 7 8 9 10

PAIRS WELL WITH	REVIEW NOTES

WOULD YOU BUY IT AGAIN?		OVERALL RATING
○ YES	○ NO	/10

WINE TASTING

NAME		ORCHARD	
ORIGIN		REGION	
TYPE		VARIETAL	
VINTAGE		ALCOHOL %	

HUES

○ STRAW	○ YELLOW	○ GOLD
○ BROWN	○ AMBER	○ COPPER
○ SALMON	○ PINK	○ RUBY
○ PURPLE	○ GARNET	○ TAWNY

INTENSITY

RED	ROSÉ	WHITE
○ PALE	○ PALE	○ PALE
○ MEDIUM	○ MEDIUM	○ MEDIUM
○ DEEP	○ DEEP	○ DEEP

AROMA

○ FRUIT	○ FLORAL	○ HERBAL
○ YEAST	○ SPICE	○ NUT
○ EARTH	○ OAK	○ VEGETAL
○	○	○

TASTE

○ CITRUS	○ BERRIES	○ COFFEE
○ MINERAL	○ SPICE	○ NUT
○ EARTH	○ BARREL	○ VANILLA
○ COCOA	○	○

SWEETNESS	ACIDITY	TANNINS
1 2 3 4 5 6 7 8 9 10	1 2 3 4 5 6 7 8 9 10	1 2 3 4 5 6 7 8 9 10

BODY	FLAVOR INTENSITY	FINISH
1 2 3 4 5 6 7 8 9 10	1 2 3 4 5 6 7 8 9 10	1 2 3 4 5 6 7 8 9 10

PAIRS WELL WITH	REVIEW NOTES

WOULD YOU BUY IT AGAIN?		OVERALL RATING
○ YES	○ NO	/10

WINE TASTING

NAME		ORCHARD	
ORIGIN		REGION	
TYPE		VARIETAL	
VINTAGE		ALCOHOL %	

HUES		
○ STRAW	○ YELLOW	○ GOLD
○ BROWN	○ AMBER	○ COPPER
○ SALMON	○ PINK	○ RUBY
○ PURPLE	○ GARNET	○ TAWNY

INTENSITY		
RED	ROSÉ	WHITE
○ PALE	○ PALE	○ PALE
○ MEDIUM	○ MEDIUM	○ MEDIUM
○ DEEP	○ DEEP	○ DEEP

AROMA		
○ FRUIT	○ FLORAL	○ HERBAL
○ YEAST	○ SPICE	○ NUT
○ EARTH	○ OAK	○ VEGETAL
○	○	○

TASTE		
○ CITRUS	○ BERRIES	○ COFFEE
○ MINERAL	○ SPICE	○ NUT
○ EARTH	○ BARREL	○ VANILLA
○ COCOA	○	○

SWEETNESS	ACIDITY	TANNINS
1 2 3 4 5 6 7 8 9 10	1 2 3 4 5 6 7 8 9 10	1 2 3 4 5 6 7 8 9 10

BODY	FLAVOR INTENSITY	FINISH
1 2 3 4 5 6 7 8 9 10	1 2 3 4 5 6 7 8 9 10	1 2 3 4 5 6 7 8 9 10

PAIRS WELL WITH	REVIEW NOTES

WOULD YOU BUY IT AGAIN?		OVERALL RATING
○ YES	○ NO	/10

WINE TASTING

NAME		ORCHARD	
ORIGIN		REGION	
TYPE		VARIETAL	
VINTAGE		ALCOHOL %	

HUES

○ STRAW	○ YELLOW	○ GOLD
○ BROWN	○ AMBER	○ COPPER
○ SALMON	○ PINK	○ RUBY
○ PURPLE	○ GARNET	○ TAWNY

INTENSITY

RED	ROSÉ	WHITE
○ PALE	○ PALE	○ PALE
○ MEDIUM	○ MEDIUM	○ MEDIUM
○ DEEP	○ DEEP	○ DEEP

AROMA

○ FRUIT	○ FLORAL	○ HERBAL
○ YEAST	○ SPICE	○ NUT
○ EARTH	○ OAK	○ VEGETAL
○	○	○

TASTE

○ CITRUS	○ BERRIES	○ COFFEE
○ MINERAL	○ SPICE	○ NUT
○ EARTH	○ BARREL	○ VANILLA
○ COCOA	○	○

SWEETNESS	ACIDITY	TANNINS
1 2 3 4 5 6 7 8 9 10	1 2 3 4 5 6 7 8 9 10	1 2 3 4 5 6 7 8 9 10

BODY	FLAVOR INTENSITY	FINISH
1 2 3 4 5 6 7 8 9 10	1 2 3 4 5 6 7 8 9 10	1 2 3 4 5 6 7 8 9 10

PAIRS WELL WITH	REVIEW NOTES

WOULD YOU BUY IT AGAIN?		OVERALL RATING
○ YES	○ NO	/10

WINE TASTING

NAME		ORCHARD	
ORIGIN		REGION	
TYPE		VARIETAL	
VINTAGE		ALCOHOL %	

HUES			INTENSITY		
			RED	ROSÉ	WHITE
○ STRAW	○ YELLOW	○ GOLD	○ PALE	○ PALE	○ PALE
○ BROWN	○ AMBER	○ COPPER	○ MEDIUM	○ MEDIUM	○ MEDIUM
○ SALMON	○ PINK	○ RUBY	○ DEEP	○ DEEP	○ DEEP
○ PURPLE	○ GARNET	○ TAWNY			

AROMA			TASTE		
○ FRUIT	○ FLORAL	○ HERBAL	○ CITRUS	○ BERRIES	○ COFFEE
○ YEAST	○ SPICE	○ NUT	○ MINERAL	○ SPICE	○ NUT
○ EARTH	○ OAK	○ VEGETAL	○ EARTH	○ BARREL	○ VANILLA
○	○	○	○ COCOA	○	○

SWEETNESS	ACIDITY	TANNINS
1 2 3 4 5 6 7 8 9 10	1 2 3 4 5 6 7 8 9 10	1 2 3 4 5 6 7 8 9 10

BODY	FLAVOR INTENSITY	FINISH
1 2 3 4 5 6 7 8 9 10	1 2 3 4 5 6 7 8 9 10	1 2 3 4 5 6 7 8 9 10

PAIRS WELL WITH	REVIEW NOTES

WOULD YOU BUY IT AGAIN?		OVERALL RATING
○ YES	○ NO	/10

WINE TASTING

NAME		ORCHARD	
ORIGIN		REGION	
TYPE		VARIETAL	
VINTAGE		ALCOHOL %	

HUES

○ STRAW	○ YELLOW	○ GOLD
○ BROWN	○ AMBER	○ COPPER
○ SALMON	○ PINK	○ RUBY
○ PURPLE	○ GARNET	○ TAWNY

INTENSITY

RED	ROSÉ	WHITE
○ PALE	○ PALE	○ PALE
○ MEDIUM	○ MEDIUM	○ MEDIUM
○ DEEP	○ DEEP	○ DEEP

AROMA

○ FRUIT	○ FLORAL	○ HERBAL
○ YEAST	○ SPICE	○ NUT
○ EARTH	○ OAK	○ VEGETAL
○	○	○

TASTE

○ CITRUS	○ BERRIES	○ COFFEE
○ MINERAL	○ SPICE	○ NUT
○ EARTH	○ BARREL	○ VANILLA
○ COCOA	○	○

SWEETNESS	ACIDITY	TANNINS
1 2 3 4 5 6 7 8 9 10	1 2 3 4 5 6 7 8 9 10	1 2 3 4 5 6 7 8 9 10

BODY	FLAVOR INTENSITY	FINISH
1 2 3 4 5 6 7 8 9 10	1 2 3 4 5 6 7 8 9 10	1 2 3 4 5 6 7 8 9 10

PAIRS WELL WITH	REVIEW NOTES

WOULD YOU BUY IT AGAIN?		OVERALL RATING
○ YES	○ NO	/10

WINE TASTING

NAME		ORCHARD	
ORIGIN		REGION	
TYPE		VARIETAL	
VINTAGE		ALCOHOL %	

HUES			INTENSITY		
			RED	ROSÉ	WHITE
○ STRAW	○ YELLOW	○ GOLD			
○ BROWN	○ AMBER	○ COPPER	○ PALE	○ PALE	○ PALE
○ SALMON	○ PINK	○ RUBY	○ MEDIUM	○ MEDIUM	○ MEDIUM
○ PURPLE	○ GARNET	○ TAWNY	○ DEEP	○ DEEP	○ DEEP

AROMA			TASTE		
○ FRUIT	○ FLORAL	○ HERBAL	○ CITRUS	○ BERRIES	○ COFFEE
○ YEAST	○ SPICE	○ NUT	○ MINERAL	○ SPICE	○ NUT
○ EARTH	○ OAK	○ VEGETAL	○ EARTH	○ BARREL	○ VANILLA
○	○	○	○ COCOA	○	○

SWEETNESS	ACIDITY	TANNINS
1 2 3 4 5 6 7 8 9 10	1 2 3 4 5 6 7 8 9 10	1 2 3 4 5 6 7 8 9 10

BODY	FLAVOR INTENSITY	FINISH
1 2 3 4 5 6 7 8 9 10	1 2 3 4 5 6 7 8 9 10	1 2 3 4 5 6 7 8 9 10

PAIRS WELL WITH	REVIEW NOTES

WOULD YOU BUY IT AGAIN?		OVERALL RATING
○ YES	○ NO	/10

WINE TASTING

NAME		ORCHARD	
ORIGIN		REGION	
TYPE		VARIETAL	
VINTAGE		ALCOHOL %	

HUES

○ STRAW	○ YELLOW	○ GOLD
○ BROWN	○ AMBER	○ COPPER
○ SALMON	○ PINK	○ RUBY
○ PURPLE	○ GARNET	○ TAWNY

INTENSITY

RED	ROSÉ	WHITE
○ PALE	○ PALE	○ PALE
○ MEDIUM	○ MEDIUM	○ MEDIUM
○ DEEP	○ DEEP	○ DEEP

AROMA

○ FRUIT	○ FLORAL	○ HERBAL
○ YEAST	○ SPICE	○ NUT
○ EARTH	○ OAK	○ VEGETAL
○	○	○

TASTE

○ CITRUS	○ BERRIES	○ COFFEE
○ MINERAL	○ SPICE	○ NUT
○ EARTH	○ BARREL	○ VANILLA
○ COCOA	○	○

SWEETNESS	ACIDITY	TANNINS
1 2 3 4 5 6 7 8 9 10	1 2 3 4 5 6 7 8 9 10	1 2 3 4 5 6 7 8 9 10

BODY	FLAVOR INTENSITY	FINISH
1 2 3 4 5 6 7 8 9 10	1 2 3 4 5 6 7 8 9 10	1 2 3 4 5 6 7 8 9 10

PAIRS WELL WITH	REVIEW NOTES

WOULD YOU BUY IT AGAIN?		OVERALL RATING
○ YES	○ NO	/10

WINE TASTING

NAME		ORCHARD	
ORIGIN		REGION	
TYPE		VARIETAL	
VINTAGE		ALCOHOL %	

HUES			INTENSITY		
			RED	ROSÉ	WHITE
○ STRAW	○ YELLOW	○ GOLD	○ PALE	○ PALE	○ PALE
○ BROWN	○ AMBER	○ COPPER	○ MEDIUM	○ MEDIUM	○ MEDIUM
○ SALMON	○ PINK	○ RUBY	○ DEEP	○ DEEP	○ DEEP
○ PURPLE	○ GARNET	○ TAWNY			

AROMA			TASTE		
○ FRUIT	○ FLORAL	○ HERBAL	○ CITRUS	○ BERRIES	○ COFFEE
○ YEAST	○ SPICE	○ NUT	○ MINERAL	○ SPICE	○ NUT
○ EARTH	○ OAK	○ VEGETAL	○ EARTH	○ BARREL	○ VANILLA
○	○	○	○ COCOA	○	○

SWEETNESS	ACIDITY	TANNINS
1 2 3 4 5 6 7 8 9 10	1 2 3 4 5 6 7 8 9 10	1 2 3 4 5 6 7 8 9 10

BODY	FLAVOR INTENSITY	FINISH
1 2 3 4 5 6 7 8 9 10	1 2 3 4 5 6 7 8 9 10	1 2 3 4 5 6 7 8 9 10

PAIRS WELL WITH	REVIEW NOTES

WOULD YOU BUY IT AGAIN?		OVERALL RATING
○ YES	○ NO	/10

WINE TASTING

NAME		ORCHARD	
ORIGIN		REGION	
TYPE		VARIETAL	
VINTAGE		ALCOHOL %	

HUES			INTENSITY		
			RED	ROSÉ	WHITE
○ STRAW	○ YELLOW	○ GOLD			
○ BROWN	○ AMBER	○ COPPER	○ PALE	○ PALE	○ PALE
○ SALMON	○ PINK	○ RUBY	○ MEDIUM	○ MEDIUM	○ MEDIUM
○ PURPLE	○ GARNET	○ TAWNY	○ DEEP	○ DEEP	○ DEEP

AROMA			TASTE		
○ FRUIT	○ FLORAL	○ HERBAL	○ CITRUS	○ BERRIES	○ COFFEE
○ YEAST	○ SPICE	○ NUT	○ MINERAL	○ SPICE	○ NUT
○ EARTH	○ OAK	○ VEGETAL	○ EARTH	○ BARREL	○ VANILLA
○	○	○	○ COCOA	○	○

SWEETNESS	ACIDITY	TANNINS
1 2 3 4 5 6 7 8 9 10	1 2 3 4 5 6 7 8 9 10	1 2 3 4 5 6 7 8 9 10

BODY	FLAVOR INTENSITY	FINISH
1 2 3 4 5 6 7 8 9 10	1 2 3 4 5 6 7 8 9 10	1 2 3 4 5 6 7 8 9 10

PAIRS WELL WITH	REVIEW NOTES

WOULD YOU BUY IT AGAIN?		OVERALL RATING
○ YES	○ NO	/10

WINE TASTING

NAME		ORCHARD	
ORIGIN		REGION	
TYPE		VARIETAL	
VINTAGE		ALCOHOL %	

HUES			INTENSITY		
			RED	ROSÉ	WHITE
○ STRAW	○ YELLOW	○ GOLD	○ PALE	○ PALE	○ PALE
○ BROWN	○ AMBER	○ COPPER	○ MEDIUM	○ MEDIUM	○ MEDIUM
○ SALMON	○ PINK	○ RUBY	○ DEEP	○ DEEP	○ DEEP
○ PURPLE	○ GARNET	○ TAWNY			

AROMA			TASTE		
○ FRUIT	○ FLORAL	○ HERBAL	○ CITRUS	○ BERRIES	○ COFFEE
○ YEAST	○ SPICE	○ NUT	○ MINERAL	○ SPICE	○ NUT
○ EARTH	○ OAK	○ VEGETAL	○ EARTH	○ BARREL	○ VANILLA
○	○	○	○ COCOA	○	○

SWEETNESS	ACIDITY	TANNINS
1 2 3 4 5 6 7 8 9 10	1 2 3 4 5 6 7 8 9 10	1 2 3 4 5 6 7 8 9 10

BODY	FLAVOR INTENSITY	FINISH
1 2 3 4 5 6 7 8 9 10	1 2 3 4 5 6 7 8 9 10	1 2 3 4 5 6 7 8 9 10

PAIRS WELL WITH	REVIEW NOTES

WOULD YOU BUY IT AGAIN?		OVERALL RATING
○ YES	○ NO	/10

WINE TASTING

NAME		ORCHARD	
ORIGIN		REGION	
TYPE		VARIETAL	
VINTAGE		ALCOHOL %	

HUES			INTENSITY		
			RED	ROSÉ	WHITE
○ STRAW	○ YELLOW	○ GOLD	○ PALE	○ PALE	○ PALE
○ BROWN	○ AMBER	○ COPPER	○ MEDIUM	○ MEDIUM	○ MEDIUM
○ SALMON	○ PINK	○ RUBY	○ DEEP	○ DEEP	○ DEEP
○ PURPLE	○ GARNET	○ TAWNY			

AROMA			TASTE		
○ FRUIT	○ FLORAL	○ HERBAL	○ CITRUS	○ BERRIES	○ COFFEE
○ YEAST	○ SPICE	○ NUT	○ MINERAL	○ SPICE	○ NUT
○ EARTH	○ OAK	○ VEGETAL	○ EARTH	○ BARREL	○ VANILLA
○	○	○	○ COCOA	○	○

SWEETNESS	ACIDITY	TANNINS
1 2 3 4 5 6 7 8 9 10	1 2 3 4 5 6 7 8 9 10	1 2 3 4 5 6 7 8 9 10

BODY	FLAVOR INTENSITY	FINISH
1 2 3 4 5 6 7 8 9 10	1 2 3 4 5 6 7 8 9 10	1 2 3 4 5 6 7 8 9 10

PAIRS WELL WITH	REVIEW NOTES

WOULD YOU BUY IT AGAIN?		OVERALL RATING
○ YES	○ NO	/10

WINE TASTING

NAME		ORCHARD	
ORIGIN		REGION	
TYPE		VARIETAL	
VINTAGE		ALCOHOL %	

HUES			INTENSITY		
			RED	ROSÉ	WHITE
○ STRAW	○ YELLOW	○ GOLD	○ PALE	○ PALE	○ PALE
○ BROWN	○ AMBER	○ COPPER	○ MEDIUM	○ MEDIUM	○ MEDIUM
○ SALMON	○ PINK	○ RUBY	○ DEEP	○ DEEP	○ DEEP
○ PURPLE	○ GARNET	○ TAWNY			

AROMA			TASTE		
○ FRUIT	○ FLORAL	○ HERBAL	○ CITRUS	○ BERRIES	○ COFFEE
○ YEAST	○ SPICE	○ NUT	○ MINERAL	○ SPICE	○ NUT
○ EARTH	○ OAK	○ VEGETAL	○ EARTH	○ BARREL	○ VANILLA
○	○	○	○ COCOA	○	○

SWEETNESS	ACIDITY	TANNINS
1 2 3 4 5 6 7 8 9 10	1 2 3 4 5 6 7 8 9 10	1 2 3 4 5 6 7 8 9 10

BODY	FLAVOR INTENSITY	FINISH
1 2 3 4 5 6 7 8 9 10	1 2 3 4 5 6 7 8 9 10	1 2 3 4 5 6 7 8 9 10

PAIRS WELL WITH	REVIEW NOTES

WOULD YOU BUY IT AGAIN?		OVERALL RATING
○ YES	○ NO	/10

WINE TASTING

NAME		ORCHARD	
ORIGIN		REGION	
TYPE		VARIETAL	
VINTAGE		ALCOHOL %	

HUES			INTENSITY		
			RED	ROSÉ	WHITE
○ STRAW	○ YELLOW	○ GOLD	○ PALE	○ PALE	○ PALE
○ BROWN	○ AMBER	○ COPPER	○ MEDIUM	○ MEDIUM	○ MEDIUM
○ SALMON	○ PINK	○ RUBY	○ DEEP	○ DEEP	○ DEEP
○ PURPLE	○ GARNET	○ TAWNY			

AROMA			TASTE		
○ FRUIT	○ FLORAL	○ HERBAL	○ CITRUS	○ BERRIES	○ COFFEE
○ YEAST	○ SPICE	○ NUT	○ MINERAL	○ SPICE	○ NUT
○ EARTH	○ OAK	○ VEGETAL	○ EARTH	○ BARREL	○ VANILLA
○	○	○	○ COCOA	○	○

SWEETNESS	ACIDITY	TANNINS
1 2 3 4 5 6 7 8 9 10	1 2 3 4 5 6 7 8 9 10	1 2 3 4 5 6 7 8 9 10

BODY	FLAVOR INTENSITY	FINISH
1 2 3 4 5 6 7 8 9 10	1 2 3 4 5 6 7 8 9 10	1 2 3 4 5 6 7 8 9 10

PAIRS WELL WITH	REVIEW NOTES

WOULD YOU BUY IT AGAIN?		OVERALL RATING
○ YES	○ NO	/10

WINE TASTING

NAME		ORCHARD	
ORIGIN		REGION	
TYPE		VARIETAL	
VINTAGE		ALCOHOL %	

HUES			INTENSITY		
○ STRAW	○ YELLOW	○ GOLD	RED	ROSÉ	WHITE
○ BROWN	○ AMBER	○ COPPER	○ PALE	○ PALE	○ PALE
○ SALMON	○ PINK	○ RUBY	○ MEDIUM	○ MEDIUM	○ MEDIUM
○ PURPLE	○ GARNET	○ TAWNY	○ DEEP	○ DEEP	○ DEEP

AROMA			TASTE		
○ FRUIT	○ FLORAL	○ HERBAL	○ CITRUS	○ BERRIES	○ COFFEE
○ YEAST	○ SPICE	○ NUT	○ MINERAL	○ SPICE	○ NUT
○ EARTH	○ OAK	○ VEGETAL	○ EARTH	○ BARREL	○ VANILLA
○	○	○	○ COCOA	○	○

SWEETNESS	ACIDITY	TANNINS
1 2 3 4 5 6 7 8 9 10	1 2 3 4 5 6 7 8 9 10	1 2 3 4 5 6 7 8 9 10

BODY	FLAVOR INTENSITY	FINISH
1 2 3 4 5 6 7 8 9 10	1 2 3 4 5 6 7 8 9 10	1 2 3 4 5 6 7 8 9 10

PAIRS WELL WITH	REVIEW NOTES

WOULD YOU BUY IT AGAIN?		OVERALL RATING
○ YES	○ NO	/10

WINE TASTING

NAME		ORCHARD	
ORIGIN		REGION	
TYPE		VARIETAL	
VINTAGE		ALCOHOL %	

HUES

○ STRAW	○ YELLOW	○ GOLD
○ BROWN	○ AMBER	○ COPPER
○ SALMON	○ PINK	○ RUBY
○ PURPLE	○ GARNET	○ TAWNY

INTENSITY

RED	ROSÉ	WHITE
○ PALE	○ PALE	○ PALE
○ MEDIUM	○ MEDIUM	○ MEDIUM
○ DEEP	○ DEEP	○ DEEP

AROMA

○ FRUIT	○ FLORAL	○ HERBAL
○ YEAST	○ SPICE	○ NUT
○ EARTH	○ OAK	○ VEGETAL
○	○	○

TASTE

○ CITRUS	○ BERRIES	○ COFFEE
○ MINERAL	○ SPICE	○ NUT
○ EARTH	○ BARREL	○ VANILLA
○ COCOA	○	○

SWEETNESS	ACIDITY	TANNINS
1 2 3 4 5 6 7 8 9 10	1 2 3 4 5 6 7 8 9 10	1 2 3 4 5 6 7 8 9 10

BODY	FLAVOR INTENSITY	FINISH
1 2 3 4 5 6 7 8 9 10	1 2 3 4 5 6 7 8 9 10	1 2 3 4 5 6 7 8 9 10

PAIRS WELL WITH	REVIEW NOTES

WOULD YOU BUY IT AGAIN?		OVERALL RATING
○ YES	○ NO	/10

WINE TASTING

NAME		ORCHARD	
ORIGIN		REGION	
TYPE		VARIETAL	
VINTAGE		ALCOHOL %	

HUES			INTENSITY		
○ STRAW	○ YELLOW	○ GOLD	RED	ROSÉ	WHITE
○ BROWN	○ AMBER	○ COPPER	○ PALE	○ PALE	○ PALE
○ SALMON	○ PINK	○ RUBY	○ MEDIUM	○ MEDIUM	○ MEDIUM
○ PURPLE	○ GARNET	○ TAWNY	○ DEEP	○ DEEP	○ DEEP

AROMA			TASTE		
○ FRUIT	○ FLORAL	○ HERBAL	○ CITRUS	○ BERRIES	○ COFFEE
○ YEAST	○ SPICE	○ NUT	○ MINERAL	○ SPICE	○ NUT
○ EARTH	○ OAK	○ VEGETAL	○ EARTH	○ BARREL	○ VANILLA
○	○	○	○ COCOA	○	○

SWEETNESS	ACIDITY	TANNINS
1 2 3 4 5 6 7 8 9 10	1 2 3 4 5 6 7 8 9 10	1 2 3 4 5 6 7 8 9 10

BODY	FLAVOR INTENSITY	FINISH
1 2 3 4 5 6 7 8 9 10	1 2 3 4 5 6 7 8 9 10	1 2 3 4 5 6 7 8 9 10

PAIRS WELL WITH	REVIEW NOTES

WOULD YOU BUY IT AGAIN?		OVERALL RATING
○ YES	○ NO	/10

WINE TASTING

NAME		ORCHARD	
ORIGIN		REGION	
TYPE		VARIETAL	
VINTAGE		ALCOHOL %	

HUES			INTENSITY		
			RED	ROSÉ	WHITE
○ STRAW	○ YELLOW	○ GOLD	○ PALE	○ PALE	○ PALE
○ BROWN	○ AMBER	○ COPPER	○ MEDIUM	○ MEDIUM	○ MEDIUM
○ SALMON	○ PINK	○ RUBY	○ DEEP	○ DEEP	○ DEEP
○ PURPLE	○ GARNET	○ TAWNY			

AROMA			TASTE		
○ FRUIT	○ FLORAL	○ HERBAL	○ CITRUS	○ BERRIES	○ COFFEE
○ YEAST	○ SPICE	○ NUT	○ MINERAL	○ SPICE	○ NUT
○ EARTH	○ OAK	○ VEGETAL	○ EARTH	○ BARREL	○ VANILLA
○	○	○	○ COCOA	○	○

SWEETNESS	ACIDITY	TANNINS
1 2 3 4 5 6 7 8 9 10	1 2 3 4 5 6 7 8 9 10	1 2 3 4 5 6 7 8 9 10

BODY	FLAVOR INTENSITY	FINISH
1 2 3 4 5 6 7 8 9 10	1 2 3 4 5 6 7 8 9 10	1 2 3 4 5 6 7 8 9 10

PAIRS WELL WITH	REVIEW NOTES

WOULD YOU BUY IT AGAIN?		OVERALL RATING
○ YES	○ NO	/10

WINE TASTING

NAME		ORCHARD	
ORIGIN		REGION	
TYPE		VARIETAL	
VINTAGE		ALCOHOL %	

HUES			INTENSITY		
○ STRAW	○ YELLOW	○ GOLD	RED	ROSÉ	WHITE
○ BROWN	○ AMBER	○ COPPER	○ PALE	○ PALE	○ PALE
○ SALMON	○ PINK	○ RUBY	○ MEDIUM	○ MEDIUM	○ MEDIUM
○ PURPLE	○ GARNET	○ TAWNY	○ DEEP	○ DEEP	○ DEEP

AROMA			TASTE		
○ FRUIT	○ FLORAL	○ HERBAL	○ CITRUS	○ BERRIES	○ COFFEE
○ YEAST	○ SPICE	○ NUT	○ MINERAL	○ SPICE	○ NUT
○ EARTH	○ OAK	○ VEGETAL	○ EARTH	○ BARREL	○ VANILLA
○	○	○	○ COCOA	○	○

SWEETNESS	ACIDITY	TANNINS
1 2 3 4 5 6 7 8 9 10	1 2 3 4 5 6 7 8 9 10	1 2 3 4 5 6 7 8 9 10

BODY	FLAVOR INTENSITY	FINISH
1 2 3 4 5 6 7 8 9 10	1 2 3 4 5 6 7 8 9 10	1 2 3 4 5 6 7 8 9 10

PAIRS WELL WITH	REVIEW NOTES

WOULD YOU BUY IT AGAIN?		OVERALL RATING
○ YES	○ NO	/10

WINE TASTING

NAME		ORCHARD	
ORIGIN		REGION	
TYPE		VARIETAL	
VINTAGE		ALCOHOL %	

HUES		
○ STRAW	○ YELLOW	○ GOLD
○ BROWN	○ AMBER	○ COPPER
○ SALMON	○ PINK	○ RUBY
○ PURPLE	○ GARNET	○ TAWNY

INTENSITY		
RED	ROSÉ	WHITE
○ PALE	○ PALE	○ PALE
○ MEDIUM	○ MEDIUM	○ MEDIUM
○ DEEP	○ DEEP	○ DEEP

AROMA		
○ FRUIT	○ FLORAL	○ HERBAL
○ YEAST	○ SPICE	○ NUT
○ EARTH	○ OAK	○ VEGETAL
○	○	○

TASTE		
○ CITRUS	○ BERRIES	○ COFFEE
○ MINERAL	○ SPICE	○ NUT
○ EARTH	○ BARREL	○ VANILLA
○ COCOA	○	○

SWEETNESS	ACIDITY	TANNINS
1 2 3 4 5 6 7 8 9 10	1 2 3 4 5 6 7 8 9 10	1 2 3 4 5 6 7 8 9 10

BODY	FLAVOR INTENSITY	FINISH
1 2 3 4 5 6 7 8 9 10	1 2 3 4 5 6 7 8 9 10	1 2 3 4 5 6 7 8 9 10

PAIRS WELL WITH	REVIEW NOTES

WOULD YOU BUY IT AGAIN?		OVERALL RATING
○ YES	○ NO	/10

WINE TASTING

NAME		ORCHARD	
ORIGIN		REGION	
TYPE		VARIETAL	
VINTAGE		ALCOHOL %	

HUES			INTENSITY		
○ STRAW	○ YELLOW	○ GOLD	RED	ROSÉ	WHITE
○ BROWN	○ AMBER	○ COPPER	○ PALE	○ PALE	○ PALE
○ SALMON	○ PINK	○ RUBY	○ MEDIUM	○ MEDIUM	○ MEDIUM
○ PURPLE	○ GARNET	○ TAWNY	○ DEEP	○ DEEP	○ DEEP

AROMA			TASTE		
○ FRUIT	○ FLORAL	○ HERBAL	○ CITRUS	○ BERRIES	○ COFFEE
○ YEAST	○ SPICE	○ NUT	○ MINERAL	○ SPICE	○ NUT
○ EARTH	○ OAK	○ VEGETAL	○ EARTH	○ BARREL	○ VANILLA
○	○	○	○ COCOA	○	○

SWEETNESS	ACIDITY	TANNINS
1 2 3 4 5 6 7 8 9 10	1 2 3 4 5 6 7 8 9 10	1 2 3 4 5 6 7 8 9 10

BODY	FLAVOR INTENSITY	FINISH
1 2 3 4 5 6 7 8 9 10	1 2 3 4 5 6 7 8 9 10	1 2 3 4 5 6 7 8 9 10

PAIRS WELL WITH	REVIEW NOTES

WOULD YOU BUY IT AGAIN?		OVERALL RATING
○ YES	○ NO	/10

WINE TASTING

NAME		ORCHARD	
ORIGIN		REGION	
TYPE		VARIETAL	
VINTAGE		ALCOHOL %	

HUES

○ STRAW	○ YELLOW	○ GOLD
○ BROWN	○ AMBER	○ COPPER
○ SALMON	○ PINK	○ RUBY
○ PURPLE	○ GARNET	○ TAWNY

INTENSITY

RED	ROSÉ	WHITE
○ PALE	○ PALE	○ PALE
○ MEDIUM	○ MEDIUM	○ MEDIUM
○ DEEP	○ DEEP	○ DEEP

AROMA

○ FRUIT	○ FLORAL	○ HERBAL
○ YEAST	○ SPICE	○ NUT
○ EARTH	○ OAK	○ VEGETAL
○	○	○

TASTE

○ CITRUS	○ BERRIES	○ COFFEE
○ MINERAL	○ SPICE	○ NUT
○ EARTH	○ BARREL	○ VANILLA
○ COCOA	○	○

SWEETNESS	ACIDITY	TANNINS
1 2 3 4 5 6 7 8 9 10	1 2 3 4 5 6 7 8 9 10	1 2 3 4 5 6 7 8 9 10

BODY	FLAVOR INTENSITY	FINISH
1 2 3 4 5 6 7 8 9 10	1 2 3 4 5 6 7 8 9 10	1 2 3 4 5 6 7 8 9 10

PAIRS WELL WITH	REVIEW NOTES

WOULD YOU BUY IT AGAIN?		OVERALL RATING
○ YES	○ NO	/10

WINE TASTING

NAME		ORCHARD	
ORIGIN		REGION	
TYPE		VARIETAL	
VINTAGE		ALCOHOL %	

HUES			INTENSITY		
			RED	ROSÉ	WHITE
○ STRAW	○ YELLOW	○ GOLD	○ PALE	○ PALE	○ PALE
○ BROWN	○ AMBER	○ COPPER	○ MEDIUM	○ MEDIUM	○ MEDIUM
○ SALMON	○ PINK	○ RUBY	○ DEEP	○ DEEP	○ DEEP
○ PURPLE	○ GARNET	○ TAWNY			

AROMA			TASTE		
○ FRUIT	○ FLORAL	○ HERBAL	○ CITRUS	○ BERRIES	○ COFFEE
○ YEAST	○ SPICE	○ NUT	○ MINERAL	○ SPICE	○ NUT
○ EARTH	○ OAK	○ VEGETAL	○ EARTH	○ BARREL	○ VANILLA
○	○	○	○ COCOA	○	○

SWEETNESS	ACIDITY	TANNINS
1 2 3 4 5 6 7 8 9 10	1 2 3 4 5 6 7 8 9 10	1 2 3 4 5 6 7 8 9 10

BODY	FLAVOR INTENSITY	FINISH
1 2 3 4 5 6 7 8 9 10	1 2 3 4 5 6 7 8 9 10	1 2 3 4 5 6 7 8 9 10

PAIRS WELL WITH	REVIEW NOTES

WOULD YOU BUY IT AGAIN?		OVERALL RATING
○ YES	○ NO	/10

WINE TASTING

NAME		ORCHARD	
ORIGIN		REGION	
TYPE		VARIETAL	
VINTAGE		ALCOHOL %	

HUES			INTENSITY		
			RED	ROSÉ	WHITE
○ STRAW	○ YELLOW	○ GOLD	○ PALE	○ PALE	○ PALE
○ BROWN	○ AMBER	○ COPPER	○ MEDIUM	○ MEDIUM	○ MEDIUM
○ SALMON	○ PINK	○ RUBY	○ DEEP	○ DEEP	○ DEEP
○ PURPLE	○ GARNET	○ TAWNY			

AROMA			TASTE		
○ FRUIT	○ FLORAL	○ HERBAL	○ CITRUS	○ BERRIES	○ COFFEE
○ YEAST	○ SPICE	○ NUT	○ MINERAL	○ SPICE	○ NUT
○ EARTH	○ OAK	○ VEGETAL	○ EARTH	○ BARREL	○ VANILLA
○	○	○	○ COCOA	○	○

SWEETNESS	ACIDITY	TANNINS
1 2 3 4 5 6 7 8 9 10	1 2 3 4 5 6 7 8 9 10	1 2 3 4 5 6 7 8 9 10

BODY	FLAVOR INTENSITY	FINISH
1 2 3 4 5 6 7 8 9 10	1 2 3 4 5 6 7 8 9 10	1 2 3 4 5 6 7 8 9 10

PAIRS WELL WITH	REVIEW NOTES

WOULD YOU BUY IT AGAIN?		OVERALL RATING
○ YES	○ NO	/10

WINE TASTING

NAME		ORCHARD	
ORIGIN		REGION	
TYPE		VARIETAL	
VINTAGE		ALCOHOL %	

HUES				INTENSITY		
				RED	ROSÉ	WHITE
○ STRAW	○ YELLOW	○ GOLD		○ PALE	○ PALE	○ PALE
○ BROWN	○ AMBER	○ COPPER		○ MEDIUM	○ MEDIUM	○ MEDIUM
○ SALMON	○ PINK	○ RUBY		○ DEEP	○ DEEP	○ DEEP
○ PURPLE	○ GARNET	○ TAWNY				

AROMA			TASTE		
○ FRUIT	○ FLORAL	○ HERBAL	○ CITRUS	○ BERRIES	○ COFFEE
○ YEAST	○ SPICE	○ NUT	○ MINERAL	○ SPICE	○ NUT
○ EARTH	○ OAK	○ VEGETAL	○ EARTH	○ BARREL	○ VANILLA
○	○	○	○ COCOA	○	○

SWEETNESS	ACIDITY	TANNINS
1 2 3 4 5 6 7 8 9 10	1 2 3 4 5 6 7 8 9 10	1 2 3 4 5 6 7 8 9 10

BODY	FLAVOR INTENSITY	FINISH
1 2 3 4 5 6 7 8 9 10	1 2 3 4 5 6 7 8 9 10	1 2 3 4 5 6 7 8 9 10

PAIRS WELL WITH	REVIEW NOTES

WOULD YOU BUY IT AGAIN?		OVERALL RATING
○ YES	○ NO	/10

WINE TASTING

NAME		ORCHARD	
ORIGIN		REGION	
TYPE		VARIETAL	
VINTAGE		ALCOHOL %	

HUES

○ STRAW	○ YELLOW	○ GOLD
○ BROWN	○ AMBER	○ COPPER
○ SALMON	○ PINK	○ RUBY
○ PURPLE	○ GARNET	○ TAWNY

INTENSITY

RED	ROSÉ	WHITE
○ PALE	○ PALE	○ PALE
○ MEDIUM	○ MEDIUM	○ MEDIUM
○ DEEP	○ DEEP	○ DEEP

AROMA

○ FRUIT	○ FLORAL	○ HERBAL
○ YEAST	○ SPICE	○ NUT
○ EARTH	○ OAK	○ VEGETAL
○	○	○

TASTE

○ CITRUS	○ BERRIES	○ COFFEE
○ MINERAL	○ SPICE	○ NUT
○ EARTH	○ BARREL	○ VANILLA
○ COCOA	○	○

SWEETNESS	ACIDITY	TANNINS
1 2 3 4 5 6 7 8 9 10	1 2 3 4 5 6 7 8 9 10	1 2 3 4 5 6 7 8 9 10

BODY	FLAVOR INTENSITY	FINISH
1 2 3 4 5 6 7 8 9 10	1 2 3 4 5 6 7 8 9 10	1 2 3 4 5 6 7 8 9 10

PAIRS WELL WITH	REVIEW NOTES

WOULD YOU BUY IT AGAIN?		OVERALL RATING
○ YES	○ NO	/10

WINE TASTING

NAME		ORCHARD	
ORIGIN		REGION	
TYPE		VARIETAL	
VINTAGE		ALCOHOL %	

HUES			INTENSITY		
			RED	ROSÉ	WHITE
○ STRAW	○ YELLOW	○ GOLD	○ PALE	○ PALE	○ PALE
○ BROWN	○ AMBER	○ COPPER	○ MEDIUM	○ MEDIUM	○ MEDIUM
○ SALMON	○ PINK	○ RUBY	○ DEEP	○ DEEP	○ DEEP
○ PURPLE	○ GARNET	○ TAWNY			

AROMA			TASTE		
○ FRUIT	○ FLORAL	○ HERBAL	○ CITRUS	○ BERRIES	○ COFFEE
○ YEAST	○ SPICE	○ NUT	○ MINERAL	○ SPICE	○ NUT
○ EARTH	○ OAK	○ VEGETAL	○ EARTH	○ BARREL	○ VANILLA
○	○	○	○ COCOA	○	○

SWEETNESS	ACIDITY	TANNINS
1 2 3 4 5 6 7 8 9 10	1 2 3 4 5 6 7 8 9 10	1 2 3 4 5 6 7 8 9 10

BODY	FLAVOR INTENSITY	FINISH
1 2 3 4 5 6 7 8 9 10	1 2 3 4 5 6 7 8 9 10	1 2 3 4 5 6 7 8 9 10

PAIRS WELL WITH	REVIEW NOTES

WOULD YOU BUY IT AGAIN?		OVERALL RATING
○ YES	○ NO	/10

WINE TASTING

NAME		ORCHARD	
ORIGIN		REGION	
TYPE		VARIETAL	
VINTAGE		ALCOHOL %	

HUES

○ STRAW	○ YELLOW	○ GOLD
○ BROWN	○ AMBER	○ COPPER
○ SALMON	○ PINK	○ RUBY
○ PURPLE	○ GARNET	○ TAWNY

INTENSITY

RED	ROSÉ	WHITE
○ PALE	○ PALE	○ PALE
○ MEDIUM	○ MEDIUM	○ MEDIUM
○ DEEP	○ DEEP	○ DEEP

AROMA

○ FRUIT	○ FLORAL	○ HERBAL
○ YEAST	○ SPICE	○ NUT
○ EARTH	○ OAK	○ VEGETAL
○	○	○

TASTE

○ CITRUS	○ BERRIES	○ COFFEE
○ MINERAL	○ SPICE	○ NUT
○ EARTH	○ BARREL	○ VANILLA
○ COCOA	○	○

SWEETNESS	ACIDITY	TANNINS
1 2 3 4 5 6 7 8 9 10	1 2 3 4 5 6 7 8 9 10	1 2 3 4 5 6 7 8 9 10

BODY	FLAVOR INTENSITY	FINISH
1 2 3 4 5 6 7 8 9 10	1 2 3 4 5 6 7 8 9 10	1 2 3 4 5 6 7 8 9 10

PAIRS WELL WITH	REVIEW NOTES

WOULD YOU BUY IT AGAIN?		OVERALL RATING
○ YES	○ NO	/10

WINE TASTING

NAME		ORCHARD	
ORIGIN		REGION	
TYPE		VARIETAL	
VINTAGE		ALCOHOL %	

HUES			INTENSITY		
			RED	ROSÉ	WHITE
○ STRAW	○ YELLOW	○ GOLD	○ PALE	○ PALE	○ PALE
○ BROWN	○ AMBER	○ COPPER	○ MEDIUM	○ MEDIUM	○ MEDIUM
○ SALMON	○ PINK	○ RUBY	○ DEEP	○ DEEP	○ DEEP
○ PURPLE	○ GARNET	○ TAWNY			

AROMA			TASTE		
○ FRUIT	○ FLORAL	○ HERBAL	○ CITRUS	○ BERRIES	○ COFFEE
○ YEAST	○ SPICE	○ NUT	○ MINERAL	○ SPICE	○ NUT
○ EARTH	○ OAK	○ VEGETAL	○ EARTH	○ BARREL	○ VANILLA
○	○	○	○ COCOA	○	○

SWEETNESS	ACIDITY	TANNINS
1 2 3 4 5 6 7 8 9 10	1 2 3 4 5 6 7 8 9 10	1 2 3 4 5 6 7 8 9 10

BODY	FLAVOR INTENSITY	FINISH
1 2 3 4 5 6 7 8 9 10	1 2 3 4 5 6 7 8 9 10	1 2 3 4 5 6 7 8 9 10

PAIRS WELL WITH	REVIEW NOTES

WOULD YOU BUY IT AGAIN?		OVERALL RATING
○ YES	○ NO	/10

WINE TASTING

NAME		ORCHARD	
ORIGIN		REGION	
TYPE		VARIETAL	
VINTAGE		ALCOHOL %	

HUES

○ STRAW	○ YELLOW	○ GOLD
○ BROWN	○ AMBER	○ COPPER
○ SALMON	○ PINK	○ RUBY
○ PURPLE	○ GARNET	○ TAWNY

INTENSITY

RED	ROSÉ	WHITE
○ PALE	○ PALE	○ PALE
○ MEDIUM	○ MEDIUM	○ MEDIUM
○ DEEP	○ DEEP	○ DEEP

AROMA

○ FRUIT	○ FLORAL	○ HERBAL
○ YEAST	○ SPICE	○ NUT
○ EARTH	○ OAK	○ VEGETAL
○	○	○

TASTE

○ CITRUS	○ BERRIES	○ COFFEE
○ MINERAL	○ SPICE	○ NUT
○ EARTH	○ BARREL	○ VANILLA
○ COCOA	○	○

SWEETNESS	ACIDITY	TANNINS
1 2 3 4 5 6 7 8 9 10	1 2 3 4 5 6 7 8 9 10	1 2 3 4 5 6 7 8 9 10

BODY	FLAVOR INTENSITY	FINISH
1 2 3 4 5 6 7 8 9 10	1 2 3 4 5 6 7 8 9 10	1 2 3 4 5 6 7 8 9 10

PAIRS WELL WITH	REVIEW NOTES

WOULD YOU BUY IT AGAIN?		OVERALL RATING
○ YES	○ NO	/10

WINE TASTING

NAME		ORCHARD	
ORIGIN		REGION	
TYPE		VARIETAL	
VINTAGE		ALCOHOL %	

HUES		
○ STRAW	○ YELLOW	○ GOLD
○ BROWN	○ AMBER	○ COPPER
○ SALMON	○ PINK	○ RUBY
○ PURPLE	○ GARNET	○ TAWNY

INTENSITY		
RED	ROSÉ	WHITE
○ PALE	○ PALE	○ PALE
○ MEDIUM	○ MEDIUM	○ MEDIUM
○ DEEP	○ DEEP	○ DEEP

AROMA		
○ FRUIT	○ FLORAL	○ HERBAL
○ YEAST	○ SPICE	○ NUT
○ EARTH	○ OAK	○ VEGETAL
○	○	○

TASTE		
○ CITRUS	○ BERRIES	○ COFFEE
○ MINERAL	○ SPICE	○ NUT
○ EARTH	○ BARREL	○ VANILLA
○ COCOA	○	○

SWEETNESS	ACIDITY	TANNINS
1 2 3 4 5 6 7 8 9 10	1 2 3 4 5 6 7 8 9 10	1 2 3 4 5 6 7 8 9 10

BODY	FLAVOR INTENSITY	FINISH
1 2 3 4 5 6 7 8 9 10	1 2 3 4 5 6 7 8 9 10	1 2 3 4 5 6 7 8 9 10

PAIRS WELL WITH	REVIEW NOTES

WOULD YOU BUY IT AGAIN?		OVERALL RATING
○ YES	○ NO	/10

WINE TASTING

NAME		ORCHARD	
ORIGIN		REGION	
TYPE		VARIETAL	
VINTAGE		ALCOHOL %	

HUES

○ STRAW	○ YELLOW	○ GOLD
○ BROWN	○ AMBER	○ COPPER
○ SALMON	○ PINK	○ RUBY
○ PURPLE	○ GARNET	○ TAWNY

INTENSITY

RED	ROSÉ	WHITE
○ PALE	○ PALE	○ PALE
○ MEDIUM	○ MEDIUM	○ MEDIUM
○ DEEP	○ DEEP	○ DEEP

AROMA

○ FRUIT	○ FLORAL	○ HERBAL
○ YEAST	○ SPICE	○ NUT
○ EARTH	○ OAK	○ VEGETAL
○	○	○

TASTE

○ CITRUS	○ BERRIES	○ COFFEE
○ MINERAL	○ SPICE	○ NUT
○ EARTH	○ BARREL	○ VANILLA
○ COCOA	○	○

SWEETNESS	ACIDITY	TANNINS
1 2 3 4 5 6 7 8 9 10	1 2 3 4 5 6 7 8 9 10	1 2 3 4 5 6 7 8 9 10

BODY	FLAVOR INTENSITY	FINISH
1 2 3 4 5 6 7 8 9 10	1 2 3 4 5 6 7 8 9 10	1 2 3 4 5 6 7 8 9 10

PAIRS WELL WITH	REVIEW NOTES

WOULD YOU BUY IT AGAIN?		OVERALL RATING
○ YES	○ NO	/10

WINE TASTING

NAME		ORCHARD	
ORIGIN		REGION	
TYPE		VARIETAL	
VINTAGE		ALCOHOL %	

HUES		
○ STRAW	○ YELLOW	○ GOLD
○ BROWN	○ AMBER	○ COPPER
○ SALMON	○ PINK	○ RUBY
○ PURPLE	○ GARNET	○ TAWNY

INTENSITY		
RED	ROSÉ	WHITE
○ PALE	○ PALE	○ PALE
○ MEDIUM	○ MEDIUM	○ MEDIUM
○ DEEP	○ DEEP	○ DEEP

AROMA		
○ FRUIT	○ FLORAL	○ HERBAL
○ YEAST	○ SPICE	○ NUT
○ EARTH	○ OAK	○ VEGETAL
○	○	○

TASTE		
○ CITRUS	○ BERRIES	○ COFFEE
○ MINERAL	○ SPICE	○ NUT
○ EARTH	○ BARREL	○ VANILLA
○ COCOA	○	○

SWEETNESS	ACIDITY	TANNINS
1 2 3 4 5 6 7 8 9 10	1 2 3 4 5 6 7 8 9 10	1 2 3 4 5 6 7 8 9 10

BODY	FLAVOR INTENSITY	FINISH
1 2 3 4 5 6 7 8 9 10	1 2 3 4 5 6 7 8 9 10	1 2 3 4 5 6 7 8 9 10

PAIRS WELL WITH	REVIEW NOTES

WOULD YOU BUY IT AGAIN?		OVERALL RATING
○ YES	○ NO	/10

WINE TASTING

NAME		ORCHARD	
ORIGIN		REGION	
TYPE		VARIETAL	
VINTAGE		ALCOHOL %	

HUES		
○ STRAW	○ YELLOW	○ GOLD
○ BROWN	○ AMBER	○ COPPER
○ SALMON	○ PINK	○ RUBY
○ PURPLE	○ GARNET	○ TAWNY

INTENSITY		
RED	ROSÉ	WHITE
○ PALE	○ PALE	○ PALE
○ MEDIUM	○ MEDIUM	○ MEDIUM
○ DEEP	○ DEEP	○ DEEP

AROMA		
○ FRUIT	○ FLORAL	○ HERBAL
○ YEAST	○ SPICE	○ NUT
○ EARTH	○ OAK	○ VEGETAL
○	○	○

TASTE		
○ CITRUS	○ BERRIES	○ COFFEE
○ MINERAL	○ SPICE	○ NUT
○ EARTH	○ BARREL	○ VANILLA
○ COCOA	○	○

SWEETNESS	ACIDITY	TANNINS
1 2 3 4 5 6 7 8 9 10	1 2 3 4 5 6 7 8 9 10	1 2 3 4 5 6 7 8 9 10

BODY	FLAVOR INTENSITY	FINISH
1 2 3 4 5 6 7 8 9 10	1 2 3 4 5 6 7 8 9 10	1 2 3 4 5 6 7 8 9 10

PAIRS WELL WITH	REVIEW NOTES

WOULD YOU BUY IT AGAIN?		OVERALL RATING
○ YES	○ NO	/10

WINE TASTING

NAME		ORCHARD	
ORIGIN		REGION	
TYPE		VARIETAL	
VINTAGE		ALCOHOL %	

HUES		
○ STRAW	○ YELLOW	○ GOLD
○ BROWN	○ AMBER	○ COPPER
○ SALMON	○ PINK	○ RUBY
○ PURPLE	○ GARNET	○ TAWNY

INTENSITY		
RED	ROSÉ	WHITE
○ PALE	○ PALE	○ PALE
○ MEDIUM	○ MEDIUM	○ MEDIUM
○ DEEP	○ DEEP	○ DEEP

AROMA		
○ FRUIT	○ FLORAL	○ HERBAL
○ YEAST	○ SPICE	○ NUT
○ EARTH	○ OAK	○ VEGETAL
○	○	○

TASTE		
○ CITRUS	○ BERRIES	○ COFFEE
○ MINERAL	○ SPICE	○ NUT
○ EARTH	○ BARREL	○ VANILLA
○ COCOA	○	○

SWEETNESS	ACIDITY	TANNINS
1 2 3 4 5 6 7 8 9 10	1 2 3 4 5 6 7 8 9 10	1 2 3 4 5 6 7 8 9 10

BODY	FLAVOR INTENSITY	FINISH
1 2 3 4 5 6 7 8 9 10	1 2 3 4 5 6 7 8 9 10	1 2 3 4 5 6 7 8 9 10

PAIRS WELL WITH	REVIEW NOTES

WOULD YOU BUY IT AGAIN?		OVERALL RATING
○ YES	○ NO	/10

WINE TASTING

NAME		ORCHARD	
ORIGIN		REGION	
TYPE		VARIETAL	
VINTAGE		ALCOHOL %	

HUES

○ STRAW	○ YELLOW	○ GOLD
○ BROWN	○ AMBER	○ COPPER
○ SALMON	○ PINK	○ RUBY
○ PURPLE	○ GARNET	○ TAWNY

INTENSITY

RED	ROSÉ	WHITE
○ PALE	○ PALE	○ PALE
○ MEDIUM	○ MEDIUM	○ MEDIUM
○ DEEP	○ DEEP	○ DEEP

AROMA

○ FRUIT	○ FLORAL	○ HERBAL
○ YEAST	○ SPICE	○ NUT
○ EARTH	○ OAK	○ VEGETAL
○	○	○

TASTE

○ CITRUS	○ BERRIES	○ COFFEE
○ MINERAL	○ SPICE	○ NUT
○ EARTH	○ BARREL	○ VANILLA
○ COCOA	○	○

SWEETNESS	ACIDITY	TANNINS
1 2 3 4 5 6 7 8 9 10	1 2 3 4 5 6 7 8 9 10	1 2 3 4 5 6 7 8 9 10

BODY	FLAVOR INTENSITY	FINISH
1 2 3 4 5 6 7 8 9 10	1 2 3 4 5 6 7 8 9 10	1 2 3 4 5 6 7 8 9 10

PAIRS WELL WITH	REVIEW NOTES

WOULD YOU BUY IT AGAIN?		OVERALL RATING
○ YES	○ NO	/10

WINE TASTING

NAME		ORCHARD	
ORIGIN		REGION	
TYPE		VARIETAL	
VINTAGE		ALCOHOL %	

HUES		
○ STRAW	○ YELLOW	○ GOLD
○ BROWN	○ AMBER	○ COPPER
○ SALMON	○ PINK	○ RUBY
○ PURPLE	○ GARNET	○ TAWNY

INTENSITY		
RED	ROSÉ	WHITE
○ PALE	○ PALE	○ PALE
○ MEDIUM	○ MEDIUM	○ MEDIUM
○ DEEP	○ DEEP	○ DEEP

AROMA		
○ FRUIT	○ FLORAL	○ HERBAL
○ YEAST	○ SPICE	○ NUT
○ EARTH	○ OAK	○ VEGETAL
○	○	○

TASTE		
○ CITRUS	○ BERRIES	○ COFFEE
○ MINERAL	○ SPICE	○ NUT
○ EARTH	○ BARREL	○ VANILLA
○ COCOA	○	○

SWEETNESS	ACIDITY	TANNINS
1 2 3 4 5 6 7 8 9 10	1 2 3 4 5 6 7 8 9 10	1 2 3 4 5 6 7 8 9 10

BODY	FLAVOR INTENSITY	FINISH
1 2 3 4 5 6 7 8 9 10	1 2 3 4 5 6 7 8 9 10	1 2 3 4 5 6 7 8 9 10

PAIRS WELL WITH	REVIEW NOTES

WOULD YOU BUY IT AGAIN?		OVERALL RATING
○ YES	○ NO	/10

WINE TASTING

NAME		ORCHARD	
ORIGIN		REGION	
TYPE		VARIETAL	
VINTAGE		ALCOHOL %	

HUES			INTENSITY		
			RED	ROSÉ	WHITE
○ STRAW	○ YELLOW	○ GOLD	○ PALE	○ PALE	○ PALE
○ BROWN	○ AMBER	○ COPPER	○ MEDIUM	○ MEDIUM	○ MEDIUM
○ SALMON	○ PINK	○ RUBY	○ DEEP	○ DEEP	○ DEEP
○ PURPLE	○ GARNET	○ TAWNY			

AROMA			TASTE		
○ FRUIT	○ FLORAL	○ HERBAL	○ CITRUS	○ BERRIES	○ COFFEE
○ YEAST	○ SPICE	○ NUT	○ MINERAL	○ SPICE	○ NUT
○ EARTH	○ OAK	○ VEGETAL	○ EARTH	○ BARREL	○ VANILLA
○	○	○	○ COCOA	○	○

SWEETNESS	ACIDITY	TANNINS
1 2 3 4 5 6 7 8 9 10	1 2 3 4 5 6 7 8 9 10	1 2 3 4 5 6 7 8 9 10

BODY	FLAVOR INTENSITY	FINISH
1 2 3 4 5 6 7 8 9 10	1 2 3 4 5 6 7 8 9 10	1 2 3 4 5 6 7 8 9 10

PAIRS WELL WITH	REVIEW NOTES

WOULD YOU BUY IT AGAIN?		OVERALL RATING
○ YES	○ NO	/10

WINE TASTING

NAME		ORCHARD	
ORIGIN		REGION	
TYPE		VARIETAL	
VINTAGE		ALCOHOL %	

HUES			INTENSITY		
			RED	ROSÉ	WHITE
○ STRAW	○ YELLOW	○ GOLD	○ PALE	○ PALE	○ PALE
○ BROWN	○ AMBER	○ COPPER	○ MEDIUM	○ MEDIUM	○ MEDIUM
○ SALMON	○ PINK	○ RUBY	○ DEEP	○ DEEP	○ DEEP
○ PURPLE	○ GARNET	○ TAWNY			

AROMA			TASTE		
○ FRUIT	○ FLORAL	○ HERBAL	○ CITRUS	○ BERRIES	○ COFFEE
○ YEAST	○ SPICE	○ NUT	○ MINERAL	○ SPICE	○ NUT
○ EARTH	○ OAK	○ VEGETAL	○ EARTH	○ BARREL	○ VANILLA
○	○	○	○ COCOA	○	○

SWEETNESS	ACIDITY	TANNINS
1 2 3 4 5 6 7 8 9 10	1 2 3 4 5 6 7 8 9 10	1 2 3 4 5 6 7 8 9 10

BODY	FLAVOR INTENSITY	FINISH
1 2 3 4 5 6 7 8 9 10	1 2 3 4 5 6 7 8 9 10	1 2 3 4 5 6 7 8 9 10

PAIRS WELL WITH	REVIEW NOTES

WOULD YOU BUY IT AGAIN?		OVERALL RATING
○ YES	○ NO	/10

WINE TASTING

NAME		ORCHARD	
ORIGIN		REGION	
TYPE		VARIETAL	
VINTAGE		ALCOHOL %	

HUES

○ STRAW	○ YELLOW	○ GOLD
○ BROWN	○ AMBER	○ COPPER
○ SALMON	○ PINK	○ RUBY
○ PURPLE	○ GARNET	○ TAWNY

INTENSITY

RED	ROSÉ	WHITE
○ PALE	○ PALE	○ PALE
○ MEDIUM	○ MEDIUM	○ MEDIUM
○ DEEP	○ DEEP	○ DEEP

AROMA

○ FRUIT	○ FLORAL	○ HERBAL
○ YEAST	○ SPICE	○ NUT
○ EARTH	○ OAK	○ VEGETAL
○	○	○

TASTE

○ CITRUS	○ BERRIES	○ COFFEE
○ MINERAL	○ SPICE	○ NUT
○ EARTH	○ BARREL	○ VANILLA
○ COCOA	○	○

SWEETNESS	ACIDITY	TANNINS
1 2 3 4 5 6 7 8 9 10	1 2 3 4 5 6 7 8 9 10	1 2 3 4 5 6 7 8 9 10

BODY	FLAVOR INTENSITY	FINISH
1 2 3 4 5 6 7 8 9 10	1 2 3 4 5 6 7 8 9 10	1 2 3 4 5 6 7 8 9 10

PAIRS WELL WITH	REVIEW NOTES

WOULD YOU BUY IT AGAIN?		OVERALL RATING
○ YES	○ NO	/10

WINE TASTING

NAME		ORCHARD	
ORIGIN		REGION	
TYPE		VARIETAL	
VINTAGE		ALCOHOL %	

HUES			INTENSITY		
○ STRAW	○ YELLOW	○ GOLD	RED	ROSÉ	WHITE
○ BROWN	○ AMBER	○ COPPER	○ PALE	○ PALE	○ PALE
○ SALMON	○ PINK	○ RUBY	○ MEDIUM	○ MEDIUM	○ MEDIUM
○ PURPLE	○ GARNET	○ TAWNY	○ DEEP	○ DEEP	○ DEEP

AROMA			TASTE		
○ FRUIT	○ FLORAL	○ HERBAL	○ CITRUS	○ BERRIES	○ COFFEE
○ YEAST	○ SPICE	○ NUT	○ MINERAL	○ SPICE	○ NUT
○ EARTH	○ OAK	○ VEGETAL	○ EARTH	○ BARREL	○ VANILLA
○	○	○	○ COCOA	○	○

SWEETNESS	ACIDITY	TANNINS
1 2 3 4 5 6 7 8 9 10	1 2 3 4 5 6 7 8 9 10	1 2 3 4 5 6 7 8 9 10

BODY	FLAVOR INTENSITY	FINISH
1 2 3 4 5 6 7 8 9 10	1 2 3 4 5 6 7 8 9 10	1 2 3 4 5 6 7 8 9 10

PAIRS WELL WITH	REVIEW NOTES

WOULD YOU BUY IT AGAIN?		OVERALL RATING
○ YES	○ NO	/10

WINE TASTING

NAME		ORCHARD	
ORIGIN		REGION	
TYPE		VARIETAL	
VINTAGE		ALCOHOL %	

HUES

○ STRAW	○ YELLOW	○ GOLD
○ BROWN	○ AMBER	○ COPPER
○ SALMON	○ PINK	○ RUBY
○ PURPLE	○ GARNET	○ TAWNY

INTENSITY

RED	ROSÉ	WHITE
○ PALE	○ PALE	○ PALE
○ MEDIUM	○ MEDIUM	○ MEDIUM
○ DEEP	○ DEEP	○ DEEP

AROMA

○ FRUIT	○ FLORAL	○ HERBAL
○ YEAST	○ SPICE	○ NUT
○ EARTH	○ OAK	○ VEGETAL
○	○	○

TASTE

○ CITRUS	○ BERRIES	○ COFFEE
○ MINERAL	○ SPICE	○ NUT
○ EARTH	○ BARREL	○ VANILLA
○ COCOA	○	○

SWEETNESS	ACIDITY	TANNINS
1 2 3 4 5 6 7 8 9 10	1 2 3 4 5 6 7 8 9 10	1 2 3 4 5 6 7 8 9 10

BODY	FLAVOR INTENSITY	FINISH
1 2 3 4 5 6 7 8 9 10	1 2 3 4 5 6 7 8 9 10	1 2 3 4 5 6 7 8 9 10

PAIRS WELL WITH	REVIEW NOTES

WOULD YOU BUY IT AGAIN?		OVERALL RATING
○ YES	○ NO	/10

WINE TASTING

NAME		ORCHARD	
ORIGIN		REGION	
TYPE		VARIETAL	
VINTAGE		ALCOHOL %	

HUES		
○ STRAW	○ YELLOW	○ GOLD
○ BROWN	○ AMBER	○ COPPER
○ SALMON	○ PINK	○ RUBY
○ PURPLE	○ GARNET	○ TAWNY

INTENSITY		
RED	ROSÉ	WHITE
○ PALE	○ PALE	○ PALE
○ MEDIUM	○ MEDIUM	○ MEDIUM
○ DEEP	○ DEEP	○ DEEP

AROMA		
○ FRUIT	○ FLORAL	○ HERBAL
○ YEAST	○ SPICE	○ NUT
○ EARTH	○ OAK	○ VEGETAL
○	○	○

TASTE		
○ CITRUS	○ BERRIES	○ COFFEE
○ MINERAL	○ SPICE	○ NUT
○ EARTH	○ BARREL	○ VANILLA
○ COCOA	○	○

SWEETNESS	ACIDITY	TANNINS
1 2 3 4 5 6 7 8 9 10	1 2 3 4 5 6 7 8 9 10	1 2 3 4 5 6 7 8 9 10

BODY	FLAVOR INTENSITY	FINISH
1 2 3 4 5 6 7 8 9 10	1 2 3 4 5 6 7 8 9 10	1 2 3 4 5 6 7 8 9 10

PAIRS WELL WITH	REVIEW NOTES

WOULD YOU BUY IT AGAIN?		OVERALL RATING
○ YES	○ NO	/10

WINE TASTING

NAME		ORCHARD	
ORIGIN		REGION	
TYPE		VARIETAL	
VINTAGE		ALCOHOL %	

HUES

○ STRAW	○ YELLOW	○ GOLD
○ BROWN	○ AMBER	○ COPPER
○ SALMON	○ PINK	○ RUBY
○ PURPLE	○ GARNET	○ TAWNY

INTENSITY

RED	ROSÉ	WHITE
○ PALE	○ PALE	○ PALE
○ MEDIUM	○ MEDIUM	○ MEDIUM
○ DEEP	○ DEEP	○ DEEP

AROMA

○ FRUIT	○ FLORAL	○ HERBAL
○ YEAST	○ SPICE	○ NUT
○ EARTH	○ OAK	○ VEGETAL
○	○	○

TASTE

○ CITRUS	○ BERRIES	○ COFFEE
○ MINERAL	○ SPICE	○ NUT
○ EARTH	○ BARREL	○ VANILLA
○ COCOA	○	○

SWEETNESS	ACIDITY	TANNINS
1 2 3 4 5 6 7 8 9 10	1 2 3 4 5 6 7 8 9 10	1 2 3 4 5 6 7 8 9 10

BODY	FLAVOR INTENSITY	FINISH
1 2 3 4 5 6 7 8 9 10	1 2 3 4 5 6 7 8 9 10	1 2 3 4 5 6 7 8 9 10

PAIRS WELL WITH	REVIEW NOTES

WOULD YOU BUY IT AGAIN?		OVERALL RATING
○ YES	○ NO	/10

WINE TASTING

NAME		ORCHARD	
ORIGIN		REGION	
TYPE		VARIETAL	
VINTAGE		ALCOHOL %	

HUES			INTENSITY		
			RED	ROSÉ	WHITE
○ STRAW	○ YELLOW	○ GOLD	○ PALE	○ PALE	○ PALE
○ BROWN	○ AMBER	○ COPPER	○ MEDIUM	○ MEDIUM	○ MEDIUM
○ SALMON	○ PINK	○ RUBY	○ DEEP	○ DEEP	○ DEEP
○ PURPLE	○ GARNET	○ TAWNY			

AROMA			TASTE		
○ FRUIT	○ FLORAL	○ HERBAL	○ CITRUS	○ BERRIES	○ COFFEE
○ YEAST	○ SPICE	○ NUT	○ MINERAL	○ SPICE	○ NUT
○ EARTH	○ OAK	○ VEGETAL	○ EARTH	○ BARREL	○ VANILLA
○	○	○	○ COCOA	○	○

SWEETNESS	ACIDITY	TANNINS
1 2 3 4 5 6 7 8 9 10	1 2 3 4 5 6 7 8 9 10	1 2 3 4 5 6 7 8 9 10

BODY	FLAVOR INTENSITY	FINISH
1 2 3 4 5 6 7 8 9 10	1 2 3 4 5 6 7 8 9 10	1 2 3 4 5 6 7 8 9 10

PAIRS WELL WITH	REVIEW NOTES

WOULD YOU BUY IT AGAIN?		OVERALL RATING
○ YES	○ NO	/10

WINE TASTING

NAME		ORCHARD	
ORIGIN		REGION	
TYPE		VARIETAL	
VINTAGE		ALCOHOL %	

HUES

○ STRAW	○ YELLOW	○ GOLD
○ BROWN	○ AMBER	○ COPPER
○ SALMON	○ PINK	○ RUBY
○ PURPLE	○ GARNET	○ TAWNY

INTENSITY

RED	ROSÉ	WHITE
○ PALE	○ PALE	○ PALE
○ MEDIUM	○ MEDIUM	○ MEDIUM
○ DEEP	○ DEEP	○ DEEP

AROMA

○ FRUIT	○ FLORAL	○ HERBAL
○ YEAST	○ SPICE	○ NUT
○ EARTH	○ OAK	○ VEGETAL
○	○	○

TASTE

○ CITRUS	○ BERRIES	○ COFFEE
○ MINERAL	○ SPICE	○ NUT
○ EARTH	○ BARREL	○ VANILLA
○ COCOA	○	○

SWEETNESS	ACIDITY	TANNINS
1 2 3 4 5 6 7 8 9 10	1 2 3 4 5 6 7 8 9 10	1 2 3 4 5 6 7 8 9 10

BODY	FLAVOR INTENSITY	FINISH
1 2 3 4 5 6 7 8 9 10	1 2 3 4 5 6 7 8 9 10	1 2 3 4 5 6 7 8 9 10

PAIRS WELL WITH	REVIEW NOTES

WOULD YOU BUY IT AGAIN?		OVERALL RATING
○ YES	○ NO	/10

WINE TASTING

NAME		ORCHARD	
ORIGIN		REGION	
TYPE		VARIETAL	
VINTAGE		ALCOHOL %	

HUES		
○ STRAW	○ YELLOW	○ GOLD
○ BROWN	○ AMBER	○ COPPER
○ SALMON	○ PINK	○ RUBY
○ PURPLE	○ GARNET	○ TAWNY

INTENSITY		
RED	ROSÉ	WHITE
○ PALE	○ PALE	○ PALE
○ MEDIUM	○ MEDIUM	○ MEDIUM
○ DEEP	○ DEEP	○ DEEP

AROMA		
○ FRUIT	○ FLORAL	○ HERBAL
○ YEAST	○ SPICE	○ NUT
○ EARTH	○ OAK	○ VEGETAL
○	○	○

TASTE		
○ CITRUS	○ BERRIES	○ COFFEE
○ MINERAL	○ SPICE	○ NUT
○ EARTH	○ BARREL	○ VANILLA
○ COCOA	○	○

SWEETNESS	ACIDITY	TANNINS
1 2 3 4 5 6 7 8 9 10	1 2 3 4 5 6 7 8 9 10	1 2 3 4 5 6 7 8 9 10

BODY	FLAVOR INTENSITY	FINISH
1 2 3 4 5 6 7 8 9 10	1 2 3 4 5 6 7 8 9 10	1 2 3 4 5 6 7 8 9 10

PAIRS WELL WITH	REVIEW NOTES

WOULD YOU BUY IT AGAIN?		OVERALL RATING
○ YES	○ NO	/10

WINE TASTING

NAME		ORCHARD	
ORIGIN		REGION	
TYPE		VARIETAL	
VINTAGE		ALCOHOL %	

HUES		
○ STRAW	○ YELLOW	○ GOLD
○ BROWN	○ AMBER	○ COPPER
○ SALMON	○ PINK	○ RUBY
○ PURPLE	○ GARNET	○ TAWNY

INTENSITY		
RED	ROSÉ	WHITE
○ PALE	○ PALE	○ PALE
○ MEDIUM	○ MEDIUM	○ MEDIUM
○ DEEP	○ DEEP	○ DEEP

AROMA		
○ FRUIT	○ FLORAL	○ HERBAL
○ YEAST	○ SPICE	○ NUT
○ EARTH	○ OAK	○ VEGETAL
○	○	○

TASTE		
○ CITRUS	○ BERRIES	○ COFFEE
○ MINERAL	○ SPICE	○ NUT
○ EARTH	○ BARREL	○ VANILLA
○ COCOA	○	○

SWEETNESS	ACIDITY	TANNINS
1 2 3 4 5 6 7 8 9 10	1 2 3 4 5 6 7 8 9 10	1 2 3 4 5 6 7 8 9 10

BODY	FLAVOR INTENSITY	FINISH
1 2 3 4 5 6 7 8 9 10	1 2 3 4 5 6 7 8 9 10	1 2 3 4 5 6 7 8 9 10

PAIRS WELL WITH	REVIEW NOTES

WOULD YOU BUY IT AGAIN?		OVERALL RATING
○ YES	○ NO	/10

WINE TASTING

NAME		ORCHARD	
ORIGIN		REGION	
TYPE		VARIETAL	
VINTAGE		ALCOHOL %	

HUES			INTENSITY		
○ STRAW	○ YELLOW	○ GOLD	RED	ROSÉ	WHITE
○ BROWN	○ AMBER	○ COPPER	○ PALE	○ PALE	○ PALE
○ SALMON	○ PINK	○ RUBY	○ MEDIUM	○ MEDIUM	○ MEDIUM
○ PURPLE	○ GARNET	○ TAWNY	○ DEEP	○ DEEP	○ DEEP

AROMA			TASTE		
○ FRUIT	○ FLORAL	○ HERBAL	○ CITRUS	○ BERRIES	○ COFFEE
○ YEAST	○ SPICE	○ NUT	○ MINERAL	○ SPICE	○ NUT
○ EARTH	○ OAK	○ VEGETAL	○ EARTH	○ BARREL	○ VANILLA
○	○	○	○ COCOA	○	○

SWEETNESS	ACIDITY	TANNINS
1 2 3 4 5 6 7 8 9 10	1 2 3 4 5 6 7 8 9 10	1 2 3 4 5 6 7 8 9 10

BODY	FLAVOR INTENSITY	FINISH
1 2 3 4 5 6 7 8 9 10	1 2 3 4 5 6 7 8 9 10	1 2 3 4 5 6 7 8 9 10

PAIRS WELL WITH	REVIEW NOTES

WOULD YOU BUY IT AGAIN?		OVERALL RATING
○ YES	○ NO	/10

WINE TASTING

NAME		ORCHARD	
ORIGIN		REGION	
TYPE		VARIETAL	
VINTAGE		ALCOHOL %	

HUES

○ STRAW	○ YELLOW	○ GOLD
○ BROWN	○ AMBER	○ COPPER
○ SALMON	○ PINK	○ RUBY
○ PURPLE	○ GARNET	○ TAWNY

INTENSITY

RED	ROSÉ	WHITE
○ PALE	○ PALE	○ PALE
○ MEDIUM	○ MEDIUM	○ MEDIUM
○ DEEP	○ DEEP	○ DEEP

AROMA

○ FRUIT	○ FLORAL	○ HERBAL
○ YEAST	○ SPICE	○ NUT
○ EARTH	○ OAK	○ VEGETAL
○	○	○

TASTE

○ CITRUS	○ BERRIES	○ COFFEE
○ MINERAL	○ SPICE	○ NUT
○ EARTH	○ BARREL	○ VANILLA
○ COCOA	○	○

SWEETNESS	ACIDITY	TANNINS
1 2 3 4 5 6 7 8 9 10	1 2 3 4 5 6 7 8 9 10	1 2 3 4 5 6 7 8 9 10

BODY	FLAVOR INTENSITY	FINISH
1 2 3 4 5 6 7 8 9 10	1 2 3 4 5 6 7 8 9 10	1 2 3 4 5 6 7 8 9 10

PAIRS WELL WITH	REVIEW NOTES

WOULD YOU BUY IT AGAIN?		OVERALL RATING
○ YES	○ NO	/10

WINE TASTING

NAME		ORCHARD	
ORIGIN		REGION	
TYPE		VARIETAL	
VINTAGE		ALCOHOL %	

HUES			INTENSITY		
			RED	ROSÉ	WHITE
○ STRAW	○ YELLOW	○ GOLD	○ PALE	○ PALE	○ PALE
○ BROWN	○ AMBER	○ COPPER	○ MEDIUM	○ MEDIUM	○ MEDIUM
○ SALMON	○ PINK	○ RUBY	○ DEEP	○ DEEP	○ DEEP
○ PURPLE	○ GARNET	○ TAWNY			

AROMA			TASTE		
○ FRUIT	○ FLORAL	○ HERBAL	○ CITRUS	○ BERRIES	○ COFFEE
○ YEAST	○ SPICE	○ NUT	○ MINERAL	○ SPICE	○ NUT
○ EARTH	○ OAK	○ VEGETAL	○ EARTH	○ BARREL	○ VANILLA
○	○	○	○ COCOA	○	○

SWEETNESS	ACIDITY	TANNINS
1 2 3 4 5 6 7 8 9 10	1 2 3 4 5 6 7 8 9 10	1 2 3 4 5 6 7 8 9 10

BODY	FLAVOR INTENSITY	FINISH
1 2 3 4 5 6 7 8 9 10	1 2 3 4 5 6 7 8 9 10	1 2 3 4 5 6 7 8 9 10

PAIRS WELL WITH	REVIEW NOTES

WOULD YOU BUY IT AGAIN?		OVERALL RATING
○ YES	○ NO	/10

WINE TASTING

NAME		ORCHARD	
ORIGIN		REGION	
TYPE		VARIETAL	
VINTAGE		ALCOHOL %	

HUES

○ STRAW	○ YELLOW	○ GOLD
○ BROWN	○ AMBER	○ COPPER
○ SALMON	○ PINK	○ RUBY
○ PURPLE	○ GARNET	○ TAWNY

INTENSITY

RED	ROSÉ	WHITE
○ PALE	○ PALE	○ PALE
○ MEDIUM	○ MEDIUM	○ MEDIUM
○ DEEP	○ DEEP	○ DEEP

AROMA

○ FRUIT	○ FLORAL	○ HERBAL
○ YEAST	○ SPICE	○ NUT
○ EARTH	○ OAK	○ VEGETAL
○	○	○

TASTE

○ CITRUS	○ BERRIES	○ COFFEE
○ MINERAL	○ SPICE	○ NUT
○ EARTH	○ BARREL	○ VANILLA
○ COCOA	○	○

SWEETNESS	ACIDITY	TANNINS
1 2 3 4 5 6 7 8 9 10	1 2 3 4 5 6 7 8 9 10	1 2 3 4 5 6 7 8 9 10

BODY	FLAVOR INTENSITY	FINISH
1 2 3 4 5 6 7 8 9 10	1 2 3 4 5 6 7 8 9 10	1 2 3 4 5 6 7 8 9 10

PAIRS WELL WITH	REVIEW NOTES

WOULD YOU BUY IT AGAIN?		OVERALL RATING
○ YES	○ NO	/10

WINE TASTING

NAME		ORCHARD	
ORIGIN		REGION	
TYPE		VARIETAL	
VINTAGE		ALCOHOL %	

HUES			INTENSITY		
			RED	ROSÉ	WHITE
○ STRAW	○ YELLOW	○ GOLD	○ PALE	○ PALE	○ PALE
○ BROWN	○ AMBER	○ COPPER	○ MEDIUM	○ MEDIUM	○ MEDIUM
○ SALMON	○ PINK	○ RUBY	○ DEEP	○ DEEP	○ DEEP
○ PURPLE	○ GARNET	○ TAWNY			

AROMA			TASTE		
○ FRUIT	○ FLORAL	○ HERBAL	○ CITRUS	○ BERRIES	○ COFFEE
○ YEAST	○ SPICE	○ NUT	○ MINERAL	○ SPICE	○ NUT
○ EARTH	○ OAK	○ VEGETAL	○ EARTH	○ BARREL	○ VANILLA
○	○	○	○ COCOA	○	○

SWEETNESS	ACIDITY	TANNINS
1 2 3 4 5 6 7 8 9 10	1 2 3 4 5 6 7 8 9 10	1 2 3 4 5 6 7 8 9 10

BODY	FLAVOR INTENSITY	FINISH
1 2 3 4 5 6 7 8 9 10	1 2 3 4 5 6 7 8 9 10	1 2 3 4 5 6 7 8 9 10

PAIRS WELL WITH	REVIEW NOTES

WOULD YOU BUY IT AGAIN?		OVERALL RATING
○ YES	○ NO	/10

WINE TASTING

NAME		ORCHARD	
ORIGIN		REGION	
TYPE		VARIETAL	
VINTAGE		ALCOHOL %	

HUES		
○ STRAW	○ YELLOW	○ GOLD
○ BROWN	○ AMBER	○ COPPER
○ SALMON	○ PINK	○ RUBY
○ PURPLE	○ GARNET	○ TAWNY

INTENSITY		
RED	ROSÉ	WHITE
○ PALE	○ PALE	○ PALE
○ MEDIUM	○ MEDIUM	○ MEDIUM
○ DEEP	○ DEEP	○ DEEP

AROMA		
○ FRUIT	○ FLORAL	○ HERBAL
○ YEAST	○ SPICE	○ NUT
○ EARTH	○ OAK	○ VEGETAL
○	○	○

TASTE		
○ CITRUS	○ BERRIES	○ COFFEE
○ MINERAL	○ SPICE	○ NUT
○ EARTH	○ BARREL	○ VANILLA
○ COCOA	○	○

SWEETNESS	ACIDITY	TANNINS
1 2 3 4 5 6 7 8 9 10	1 2 3 4 5 6 7 8 9 10	1 2 3 4 5 6 7 8 9 10

BODY	FLAVOR INTENSITY	FINISH
1 2 3 4 5 6 7 8 9 10	1 2 3 4 5 6 7 8 9 10	1 2 3 4 5 6 7 8 9 10

PAIRS WELL WITH	REVIEW NOTES

WOULD YOU BUY IT AGAIN?		OVERALL RATING
○ YES	○ NO	/10

WINE TASTING

NAME		ORCHARD	
ORIGIN		REGION	
TYPE		VARIETAL	
VINTAGE		ALCOHOL %	

HUES			INTENSITY		
			RED	ROSÉ	WHITE
○ STRAW	○ YELLOW	○ GOLD	○ PALE	○ PALE	○ PALE
○ BROWN	○ AMBER	○ COPPER	○ MEDIUM	○ MEDIUM	○ MEDIUM
○ SALMON	○ PINK	○ RUBY	○ DEEP	○ DEEP	○ DEEP
○ PURPLE	○ GARNET	○ TAWNY			

AROMA			TASTE		
○ FRUIT	○ FLORAL	○ HERBAL	○ CITRUS	○ BERRIES	○ COFFEE
○ YEAST	○ SPICE	○ NUT	○ MINERAL	○ SPICE	○ NUT
○ EARTH	○ OAK	○ VEGETAL	○ EARTH	○ BARREL	○ VANILLA
○	○	○	○ COCOA	○	○

SWEETNESS	ACIDITY	TANNINS
1 2 3 4 5 6 7 8 9 10	1 2 3 4 5 6 7 8 9 10	1 2 3 4 5 6 7 8 9 10

BODY	FLAVOR INTENSITY	FINISH
1 2 3 4 5 6 7 8 9 10	1 2 3 4 5 6 7 8 9 10	1 2 3 4 5 6 7 8 9 10

PAIRS WELL WITH	REVIEW NOTES

WOULD YOU BUY IT AGAIN?		OVERALL RATING
○ YES	○ NO	/10

WINE TASTING

NAME		ORCHARD	
ORIGIN		REGION	
TYPE		VARIETAL	
VINTAGE		ALCOHOL %	

HUES

○ STRAW	○ YELLOW	○ GOLD
○ BROWN	○ AMBER	○ COPPER
○ SALMON	○ PINK	○ RUBY
○ PURPLE	○ GARNET	○ TAWNY

INTENSITY

RED	ROSÉ	WHITE
○ PALE	○ PALE	○ PALE
○ MEDIUM	○ MEDIUM	○ MEDIUM
○ DEEP	○ DEEP	○ DEEP

AROMA

○ FRUIT	○ FLORAL	○ HERBAL
○ YEAST	○ SPICE	○ NUT
○ EARTH	○ OAK	○ VEGETAL
○	○	○

TASTE

○ CITRUS	○ BERRIES	○ COFFEE
○ MINERAL	○ SPICE	○ NUT
○ EARTH	○ BARREL	○ VANILLA
○ COCOA	○	○

SWEETNESS	ACIDITY	TANNINS
1 2 3 4 5 6 7 8 9 10	1 2 3 4 5 6 7 8 9 10	1 2 3 4 5 6 7 8 9 10

BODY	FLAVOR INTENSITY	FINISH
1 2 3 4 5 6 7 8 9 10	1 2 3 4 5 6 7 8 9 10	1 2 3 4 5 6 7 8 9 10

PAIRS WELL WITH	REVIEW NOTES

WOULD YOU BUY IT AGAIN?		OVERALL RATING
○ YES	○ NO	/10

WINE TASTING

NAME		ORCHARD	
ORIGIN		REGION	
TYPE		VARIETAL	
VINTAGE		ALCOHOL %	

HUES		
○ STRAW	○ YELLOW	○ GOLD
○ BROWN	○ AMBER	○ COPPER
○ SALMON	○ PINK	○ RUBY
○ PURPLE	○ GARNET	○ TAWNY

INTENSITY		
RED	ROSÉ	WHITE
○ PALE	○ PALE	○ PALE
○ MEDIUM	○ MEDIUM	○ MEDIUM
○ DEEP	○ DEEP	○ DEEP

AROMA		
○ FRUIT	○ FLORAL	○ HERBAL
○ YEAST	○ SPICE	○ NUT
○ EARTH	○ OAK	○ VEGETAL
○	○	○

TASTE		
○ CITRUS	○ BERRIES	○ COFFEE
○ MINERAL	○ SPICE	○ NUT
○ EARTH	○ BARREL	○ VANILLA
○ COCOA	○	○

SWEETNESS	ACIDITY	TANNINS
1 2 3 4 5 6 7 8 9 10	1 2 3 4 5 6 7 8 9 10	1 2 3 4 5 6 7 8 9 10

BODY	FLAVOR INTENSITY	FINISH
1 2 3 4 5 6 7 8 9 10	1 2 3 4 5 6 7 8 9 10	1 2 3 4 5 6 7 8 9 10

PAIRS WELL WITH	REVIEW NOTES

WOULD YOU BUY IT AGAIN?		OVERALL RATING
○ YES	○ NO	/10

WINE TASTING

NAME		ORCHARD	
ORIGIN		REGION	
TYPE		VARIETAL	
VINTAGE		ALCOHOL %	

HUES

○ STRAW	○ YELLOW	○ GOLD
○ BROWN	○ AMBER	○ COPPER
○ SALMON	○ PINK	○ RUBY
○ PURPLE	○ GARNET	○ TAWNY

INTENSITY

RED	ROSÉ	WHITE
○ PALE	○ PALE	○ PALE
○ MEDIUM	○ MEDIUM	○ MEDIUM
○ DEEP	○ DEEP	○ DEEP

AROMA

○ FRUIT	○ FLORAL	○ HERBAL
○ YEAST	○ SPICE	○ NUT
○ EARTH	○ OAK	○ VEGETAL
○	○	○

TASTE

○ CITRUS	○ BERRIES	○ COFFEE
○ MINERAL	○ SPICE	○ NUT
○ EARTH	○ BARREL	○ VANILLA
○ COCOA	○	○

SWEETNESS	ACIDITY	TANNINS
1 2 3 4 5 6 7 8 9 10	1 2 3 4 5 6 7 8 9 10	1 2 3 4 5 6 7 8 9 10

BODY	FLAVOR INTENSITY	FINISH
1 2 3 4 5 6 7 8 9 10	1 2 3 4 5 6 7 8 9 10	1 2 3 4 5 6 7 8 9 10

PAIRS WELL WITH	REVIEW NOTES

WOULD YOU BUY IT AGAIN?		OVERALL RATING
○ YES	○ NO	/10

WINE TASTING

NAME		ORCHARD	
ORIGIN		REGION	
TYPE		VARIETAL	
VINTAGE		ALCOHOL %	

HUES		
○ STRAW	○ YELLOW	○ GOLD
○ BROWN	○ AMBER	○ COPPER
○ SALMON	○ PINK	○ RUBY
○ PURPLE	○ GARNET	○ TAWNY

INTENSITY		
RED	ROSÉ	WHITE
○ PALE	○ PALE	○ PALE
○ MEDIUM	○ MEDIUM	○ MEDIUM
○ DEEP	○ DEEP	○ DEEP

AROMA		
○ FRUIT	○ FLORAL	○ HERBAL
○ YEAST	○ SPICE	○ NUT
○ EARTH	○ OAK	○ VEGETAL
○	○	○

TASTE		
○ CITRUS	○ BERRIES	○ COFFEE
○ MINERAL	○ SPICE	○ NUT
○ EARTH	○ BARREL	○ VANILLA
○ COCOA	○	○

SWEETNESS	ACIDITY	TANNINS
1 2 3 4 5 6 7 8 9 10	1 2 3 4 5 6 7 8 9 10	1 2 3 4 5 6 7 8 9 10

BODY	FLAVOR INTENSITY	FINISH
1 2 3 4 5 6 7 8 9 10	1 2 3 4 5 6 7 8 9 10	1 2 3 4 5 6 7 8 9 10

PAIRS WELL WITH	REVIEW NOTES

WOULD YOU BUY IT AGAIN?		OVERALL RATING
○ YES	○ NO	/10

WINE TASTING

NAME		ORCHARD	
ORIGIN		REGION	
TYPE		VARIETAL	
VINTAGE		ALCOHOL %	

HUES			INTENSITY		
			RED	ROSÉ	WHITE
○ STRAW	○ YELLOW	○ GOLD	○ PALE	○ PALE	○ PALE
○ BROWN	○ AMBER	○ COPPER	○ MEDIUM	○ MEDIUM	○ MEDIUM
○ SALMON	○ PINK	○ RUBY	○ DEEP	○ DEEP	○ DEEP
○ PURPLE	○ GARNET	○ TAWNY			

AROMA			TASTE		
○ FRUIT	○ FLORAL	○ HERBAL	○ CITRUS	○ BERRIES	○ COFFEE
○ YEAST	○ SPICE	○ NUT	○ MINERAL	○ SPICE	○ NUT
○ EARTH	○ OAK	○ VEGETAL	○ EARTH	○ BARREL	○ VANILLA
○	○	○	○ COCOA	○	○

SWEETNESS	ACIDITY	TANNINS
1 2 3 4 5 6 7 8 9 10	1 2 3 4 5 6 7 8 9 10	1 2 3 4 5 6 7 8 9 10

BODY	FLAVOR INTENSITY	FINISH
1 2 3 4 5 6 7 8 9 10	1 2 3 4 5 6 7 8 9 10	1 2 3 4 5 6 7 8 9 10

PAIRS WELL WITH	REVIEW NOTES

WOULD YOU BUY IT AGAIN?		OVERALL RATING
○ YES	○ NO	/10

WINE TASTING

NAME		ORCHARD	
ORIGIN		REGION	
TYPE		VARIETAL	
VINTAGE		ALCOHOL %	

HUES			INTENSITY		
			RED	ROSÉ	WHITE
○ STRAW	○ YELLOW	○ GOLD			
○ BROWN	○ AMBER	○ COPPER	○ PALE	○ PALE	○ PALE
○ SALMON	○ PINK	○ RUBY	○ MEDIUM	○ MEDIUM	○ MEDIUM
○ PURPLE	○ GARNET	○ TAWNY	○ DEEP	○ DEEP	○ DEEP

AROMA			TASTE		
○ FRUIT	○ FLORAL	○ HERBAL	○ CITRUS	○ BERRIES	○ COFFEE
○ YEAST	○ SPICE	○ NUT	○ MINERAL	○ SPICE	○ NUT
○ EARTH	○ OAK	○ VEGETAL	○ EARTH	○ BARREL	○ VANILLA
○	○	○	○ COCOA	○	○

SWEETNESS	ACIDITY	TANNINS
1 2 3 4 5 6 7 8 9 10	1 2 3 4 5 6 7 8 9 10	1 2 3 4 5 6 7 8 9 10

BODY	FLAVOR INTENSITY	FINISH
1 2 3 4 5 6 7 8 9 10	1 2 3 4 5 6 7 8 9 10	1 2 3 4 5 6 7 8 9 10

PAIRS WELL WITH	REVIEW NOTES

WOULD YOU BUY IT AGAIN?		OVERALL RATING
○ YES	○ NO	/10

WINE TASTING

NAME		ORCHARD	
ORIGIN		REGION	
TYPE		VARIETAL	
VINTAGE		ALCOHOL %	

HUES

○ STRAW	○ YELLOW	○ GOLD
○ BROWN	○ AMBER	○ COPPER
○ SALMON	○ PINK	○ RUBY
○ PURPLE	○ GARNET	○ TAWNY

INTENSITY

RED	ROSÉ	WHITE
○ PALE	○ PALE	○ PALE
○ MEDIUM	○ MEDIUM	○ MEDIUM
○ DEEP	○ DEEP	○ DEEP

AROMA

○ FRUIT	○ FLORAL	○ HERBAL
○ YEAST	○ SPICE	○ NUT
○ EARTH	○ OAK	○ VEGETAL
○	○	○

TASTE

○ CITRUS	○ BERRIES	○ COFFEE
○ MINERAL	○ SPICE	○ NUT
○ EARTH	○ BARREL	○ VANILLA
○ COCOA	○	○

SWEETNESS	ACIDITY	TANNINS
1 2 3 4 5 6 7 8 9 10	1 2 3 4 5 6 7 8 9 10	1 2 3 4 5 6 7 8 9 10

BODY	FLAVOR INTENSITY	FINISH
1 2 3 4 5 6 7 8 9 10	1 2 3 4 5 6 7 8 9 10	1 2 3 4 5 6 7 8 9 10

PAIRS WELL WITH	REVIEW NOTES

WOULD YOU BUY IT AGAIN?		OVERALL RATING
○ YES	○ NO	/10

WINE TASTING

NAME		ORCHARD	
ORIGIN		REGION	
TYPE		VARIETAL	
VINTAGE		ALCOHOL %	

HUES

○ STRAW	○ YELLOW	○ GOLD
○ BROWN	○ AMBER	○ COPPER
○ SALMON	○ PINK	○ RUBY
○ PURPLE	○ GARNET	○ TAWNY

INTENSITY

RED	ROSÉ	WHITE
○ PALE	○ PALE	○ PALE
○ MEDIUM	○ MEDIUM	○ MEDIUM
○ DEEP	○ DEEP	○ DEEP

AROMA

○ FRUIT	○ FLORAL	○ HERBAL
○ YEAST	○ SPICE	○ NUT
○ EARTH	○ OAK	○ VEGETAL
○	○	○

TASTE

○ CITRUS	○ BERRIES	○ COFFEE
○ MINERAL	○ SPICE	○ NUT
○ EARTH	○ BARREL	○ VANILLA
○ COCOA	○	○

SWEETNESS	ACIDITY	TANNINS
1 2 3 4 5 6 7 8 9 10	1 2 3 4 5 6 7 8 9 10	1 2 3 4 5 6 7 8 9 10

BODY	FLAVOR INTENSITY	FINISH
1 2 3 4 5 6 7 8 9 10	1 2 3 4 5 6 7 8 9 10	1 2 3 4 5 6 7 8 9 10

PAIRS WELL WITH	REVIEW NOTES

WOULD YOU BUY IT AGAIN?		OVERALL RATING
○ YES	○ NO	/10

WINE TASTING

NAME		ORCHARD	
ORIGIN		REGION	
TYPE		VARIETAL	
VINTAGE		ALCOHOL %	

HUES

○ STRAW	○ YELLOW	○ GOLD
○ BROWN	○ AMBER	○ COPPER
○ SALMON	○ PINK	○ RUBY
○ PURPLE	○ GARNET	○ TAWNY

INTENSITY

RED	ROSÉ	WHITE
○ PALE	○ PALE	○ PALE
○ MEDIUM	○ MEDIUM	○ MEDIUM
○ DEEP	○ DEEP	○ DEEP

AROMA

○ FRUIT	○ FLORAL	○ HERBAL
○ YEAST	○ SPICE	○ NUT
○ EARTH	○ OAK	○ VEGETAL
○	○	○

TASTE

○ CITRUS	○ BERRIES	○ COFFEE
○ MINERAL	○ SPICE	○ NUT
○ EARTH	○ BARREL	○ VANILLA
○ COCOA	○	○

SWEETNESS	ACIDITY	TANNINS
1 2 3 4 5 6 7 8 9 10	1 2 3 4 5 6 7 8 9 10	1 2 3 4 5 6 7 8 9 10

BODY	FLAVOR INTENSITY	FINISH
1 2 3 4 5 6 7 8 9 10	1 2 3 4 5 6 7 8 9 10	1 2 3 4 5 6 7 8 9 10

PAIRS WELL WITH	REVIEW NOTES

WOULD YOU BUY IT AGAIN?		OVERALL RATING
○ YES	○ NO	/10

WINE TASTING

NAME		ORCHARD	
ORIGIN		REGION	
TYPE		VARIETAL	
VINTAGE		ALCOHOL %	

HUES		
○ STRAW	○ YELLOW	○ GOLD
○ BROWN	○ AMBER	○ COPPER
○ SALMON	○ PINK	○ RUBY
○ PURPLE	○ GARNET	○ TAWNY

INTENSITY		
RED	ROSÉ	WHITE
○ PALE	○ PALE	○ PALE
○ MEDIUM	○ MEDIUM	○ MEDIUM
○ DEEP	○ DEEP	○ DEEP

AROMA		
○ FRUIT	○ FLORAL	○ HERBAL
○ YEAST	○ SPICE	○ NUT
○ EARTH	○ OAK	○ VEGETAL
○	○	○

TASTE		
○ CITRUS	○ BERRIES	○ COFFEE
○ MINERAL	○ SPICE	○ NUT
○ EARTH	○ BARREL	○ VANILLA
○ COCOA	○	○

SWEETNESS	ACIDITY	TANNINS
1 2 3 4 5 6 7 8 9 10	1 2 3 4 5 6 7 8 9 10	1 2 3 4 5 6 7 8 9 10

BODY	FLAVOR INTENSITY	FINISH
1 2 3 4 5 6 7 8 9 10	1 2 3 4 5 6 7 8 9 10	1 2 3 4 5 6 7 8 9 10

PAIRS WELL WITH	REVIEW NOTES

WOULD YOU BUY IT AGAIN?		OVERALL RATING
○ YES	○ NO	/10

WINE TASTING

NAME		ORCHARD	
ORIGIN		REGION	
TYPE		VARIETAL	
VINTAGE		ALCOHOL %	

HUES

○ STRAW	○ YELLOW	○ GOLD
○ BROWN	○ AMBER	○ COPPER
○ SALMON	○ PINK	○ RUBY
○ PURPLE	○ GARNET	○ TAWNY

INTENSITY

RED	ROSÉ	WHITE
○ PALE	○ PALE	○ PALE
○ MEDIUM	○ MEDIUM	○ MEDIUM
○ DEEP	○ DEEP	○ DEEP

AROMA

○ FRUIT	○ FLORAL	○ HERBAL
○ YEAST	○ SPICE	○ NUT
○ EARTH	○ OAK	○ VEGETAL
○	○	○

TASTE

○ CITRUS	○ BERRIES	○ COFFEE
○ MINERAL	○ SPICE	○ NUT
○ EARTH	○ BARREL	○ VANILLA
○ COCOA	○	○

SWEETNESS	ACIDITY	TANNINS
1 2 3 4 5 6 7 8 9 10	1 2 3 4 5 6 7 8 9 10	1 2 3 4 5 6 7 8 9 10

BODY	FLAVOR INTENSITY	FINISH
1 2 3 4 5 6 7 8 9 10	1 2 3 4 5 6 7 8 9 10	1 2 3 4 5 6 7 8 9 10

PAIRS WELL WITH	REVIEW NOTES

WOULD YOU BUY IT AGAIN?		OVERALL RATING
○ YES	○ NO	/10

WINE TASTING

NAME		ORCHARD	
ORIGIN		REGION	
TYPE		VARIETAL	
VINTAGE		ALCOHOL %	

HUES			INTENSITY		
			RED	ROSÉ	WHITE
○ STRAW	○ YELLOW	○ GOLD	○ PALE	○ PALE	○ PALE
○ BROWN	○ AMBER	○ COPPER	○ MEDIUM	○ MEDIUM	○ MEDIUM
○ SALMON	○ PINK	○ RUBY	○ DEEP	○ DEEP	○ DEEP
○ PURPLE	○ GARNET	○ TAWNY			

AROMA			TASTE		
○ FRUIT	○ FLORAL	○ HERBAL	○ CITRUS	○ BERRIES	○ COFFEE
○ YEAST	○ SPICE	○ NUT	○ MINERAL	○ SPICE	○ NUT
○ EARTH	○ OAK	○ VEGETAL	○ EARTH	○ BARREL	○ VANILLA
○	○	○	○ COCOA	○	○

SWEETNESS	ACIDITY	TANNINS
1 2 3 4 5 6 7 8 9 10	1 2 3 4 5 6 7 8 9 10	1 2 3 4 5 6 7 8 9 10

BODY	FLAVOR INTENSITY	FINISH
1 2 3 4 5 6 7 8 9 10	1 2 3 4 5 6 7 8 9 10	1 2 3 4 5 6 7 8 9 10

PAIRS WELL WITH	REVIEW NOTES

WOULD YOU BUY IT AGAIN?		OVERALL RATING
○ YES	○ NO	/10

WINE TASTING

NAME		ORCHARD	
ORIGIN		REGION	
TYPE		VARIETAL	
VINTAGE		ALCOHOL %	

HUES

○ STRAW	○ YELLOW	○ GOLD
○ BROWN	○ AMBER	○ COPPER
○ SALMON	○ PINK	○ RUBY
○ PURPLE	○ GARNET	○ TAWNY

INTENSITY

RED	ROSÉ	WHITE
○ PALE	○ PALE	○ PALE
○ MEDIUM	○ MEDIUM	○ MEDIUM
○ DEEP	○ DEEP	○ DEEP

AROMA

○ FRUIT	○ FLORAL	○ HERBAL
○ YEAST	○ SPICE	○ NUT
○ EARTH	○ OAK	○ VEGETAL
○	○	○

TASTE

○ CITRUS	○ BERRIES	○ COFFEE
○ MINERAL	○ SPICE	○ NUT
○ EARTH	○ BARREL	○ VANILLA
○ COCOA	○	○

SWEETNESS	ACIDITY	TANNINS
1 2 3 4 5 6 7 8 9 10	1 2 3 4 5 6 7 8 9 10	1 2 3 4 5 6 7 8 9 10

BODY	FLAVOR INTENSITY	FINISH
1 2 3 4 5 6 7 8 9 10	1 2 3 4 5 6 7 8 9 10	1 2 3 4 5 6 7 8 9 10

PAIRS WELL WITH	REVIEW NOTES

WOULD YOU BUY IT AGAIN?		OVERALL RATING
○ YES	○ NO	/10

WINE TASTING

NAME		ORCHARD	
ORIGIN		REGION	
TYPE		VARIETAL	
VINTAGE		ALCOHOL %	

HUES			INTENSITY		
○ STRAW	○ YELLOW	○ GOLD	RED	ROSÉ	WHITE
○ BROWN	○ AMBER	○ COPPER	○ PALE	○ PALE	○ PALE
○ SALMON	○ PINK	○ RUBY	○ MEDIUM	○ MEDIUM	○ MEDIUM
○ PURPLE	○ GARNET	○ TAWNY	○ DEEP	○ DEEP	○ DEEP

AROMA			TASTE		
○ FRUIT	○ FLORAL	○ HERBAL	○ CITRUS	○ BERRIES	○ COFFEE
○ YEAST	○ SPICE	○ NUT	○ MINERAL	○ SPICE	○ NUT
○ EARTH	○ OAK	○ VEGETAL	○ EARTH	○ BARREL	○ VANILLA
○	○	○	○ COCOA	○	○

SWEETNESS	ACIDITY	TANNINS
1 2 3 4 5 6 7 8 9 10	1 2 3 4 5 6 7 8 9 10	1 2 3 4 5 6 7 8 9 10

BODY	FLAVOR INTENSITY	FINISH
1 2 3 4 5 6 7 8 9 10	1 2 3 4 5 6 7 8 9 10	1 2 3 4 5 6 7 8 9 10

PAIRS WELL WITH	REVIEW NOTES

WOULD YOU BUY IT AGAIN?		OVERALL RATING
○ YES	○ NO	/10

WINE TASTING

NAME		ORCHARD	
ORIGIN		REGION	
TYPE		VARIETAL	
VINTAGE		ALCOHOL %	

HUES			INTENSITY		
			RED	ROSÉ	WHITE
○ STRAW	○ YELLOW	○ GOLD	○ PALE	○ PALE	○ PALE
○ BROWN	○ AMBER	○ COPPER	○ MEDIUM	○ MEDIUM	○ MEDIUM
○ SALMON	○ PINK	○ RUBY	○ DEEP	○ DEEP	○ DEEP
○ PURPLE	○ GARNET	○ TAWNY			

AROMA			TASTE		
○ FRUIT	○ FLORAL	○ HERBAL	○ CITRUS	○ BERRIES	○ COFFEE
○ YEAST	○ SPICE	○ NUT	○ MINERAL	○ SPICE	○ NUT
○ EARTH	○ OAK	○ VEGETAL	○ EARTH	○ BARREL	○ VANILLA
○	○	○	○ COCOA	○	○

SWEETNESS	ACIDITY	TANNINS
1 2 3 4 5 6 7 8 9 10	1 2 3 4 5 6 7 8 9 10	1 2 3 4 5 6 7 8 9 10

BODY	FLAVOR INTENSITY	FINISH
1 2 3 4 5 6 7 8 9 10	1 2 3 4 5 6 7 8 9 10	1 2 3 4 5 6 7 8 9 10

PAIRS WELL WITH	REVIEW NOTES

WOULD YOU BUY IT AGAIN?		OVERALL RATING
○ YES	○ NO	/10

WINE TASTING

NAME		ORCHARD	
ORIGIN		REGION	
TYPE		VARIETAL	
VINTAGE		ALCOHOL %	

HUES			INTENSITY		
			RED	ROSÉ	WHITE
○ STRAW	○ YELLOW	○ GOLD	○ PALE	○ PALE	○ PALE
○ BROWN	○ AMBER	○ COPPER	○ MEDIUM	○ MEDIUM	○ MEDIUM
○ SALMON	○ PINK	○ RUBY	○ DEEP	○ DEEP	○ DEEP
○ PURPLE	○ GARNET	○ TAWNY			

AROMA			TASTE		
○ FRUIT	○ FLORAL	○ HERBAL	○ CITRUS	○ BERRIES	○ COFFEE
○ YEAST	○ SPICE	○ NUT	○ MINERAL	○ SPICE	○ NUT
○ EARTH	○ OAK	○ VEGETAL	○ EARTH	○ BARREL	○ VANILLA
○	○	○	○ COCOA	○	○

SWEETNESS	ACIDITY	TANNINS
1 2 3 4 5 6 7 8 9 10	1 2 3 4 5 6 7 8 9 10	1 2 3 4 5 6 7 8 9 10

BODY	FLAVOR INTENSITY	FINISH
1 2 3 4 5 6 7 8 9 10	1 2 3 4 5 6 7 8 9 10	1 2 3 4 5 6 7 8 9 10

PAIRS WELL WITH	REVIEW NOTES

WOULD YOU BUY IT AGAIN?		OVERALL RATING
○ YES	○ NO	/10

WINE TASTING

NAME		ORCHARD	
ORIGIN		REGION	
TYPE		VARIETAL	
VINTAGE		ALCOHOL %	

HUES

○ STRAW	○ YELLOW	○ GOLD
○ BROWN	○ AMBER	○ COPPER
○ SALMON	○ PINK	○ RUBY
○ PURPLE	○ GARNET	○ TAWNY

INTENSITY

RED	ROSÉ	WHITE
○ PALE	○ PALE	○ PALE
○ MEDIUM	○ MEDIUM	○ MEDIUM
○ DEEP	○ DEEP	○ DEEP

AROMA

○ FRUIT	○ FLORAL	○ HERBAL
○ YEAST	○ SPICE	○ NUT
○ EARTH	○ OAK	○ VEGETAL
○	○	○

TASTE

○ CITRUS	○ BERRIES	○ COFFEE
○ MINERAL	○ SPICE	○ NUT
○ EARTH	○ BARREL	○ VANILLA
○ COCOA	○	○

SWEETNESS	ACIDITY	TANNINS
1 2 3 4 5 6 7 8 9 10	1 2 3 4 5 6 7 8 9 10	1 2 3 4 5 6 7 8 9 10

BODY	FLAVOR INTENSITY	FINISH
1 2 3 4 5 6 7 8 9 10	1 2 3 4 5 6 7 8 9 10	1 2 3 4 5 6 7 8 9 10

PAIRS WELL WITH	REVIEW NOTES

WOULD YOU BUY IT AGAIN?		OVERALL RATING
○ YES	○ NO	/10

WINE TASTING

NAME		ORCHARD	
ORIGIN		REGION	
TYPE		VARIETAL	
VINTAGE		ALCOHOL %	

HUES			INTENSITY		
○ STRAW	○ YELLOW	○ GOLD	RED	ROSÉ	WHITE
○ BROWN	○ AMBER	○ COPPER	○ PALE	○ PALE	○ PALE
○ SALMON	○ PINK	○ RUBY	○ MEDIUM	○ MEDIUM	○ MEDIUM
○ PURPLE	○ GARNET	○ TAWNY	○ DEEP	○ DEEP	○ DEEP

AROMA			TASTE		
○ FRUIT	○ FLORAL	○ HERBAL	○ CITRUS	○ BERRIES	○ COFFEE
○ YEAST	○ SPICE	○ NUT	○ MINERAL	○ SPICE	○ NUT
○ EARTH	○ OAK	○ VEGETAL	○ EARTH	○ BARREL	○ VANILLA
○	○	○	○ COCOA	○	○

SWEETNESS	ACIDITY	TANNINS
1 2 3 4 5 6 7 8 9 10	1 2 3 4 5 6 7 8 9 10	1 2 3 4 5 6 7 8 9 10

BODY	FLAVOR INTENSITY	FINISH
1 2 3 4 5 6 7 8 9 10	1 2 3 4 5 6 7 8 9 10	1 2 3 4 5 6 7 8 9 10

PAIRS WELL WITH	REVIEW NOTES

WOULD YOU BUY IT AGAIN?		OVERALL RATING
○ YES	○ NO	/10

WINE TASTING

NAME		ORCHARD	
ORIGIN		REGION	
TYPE		VARIETAL	
VINTAGE		ALCOHOL %	

HUES				INTENSITY		
○ STRAW	○ YELLOW	○ GOLD		RED	ROSÉ	WHITE
○ BROWN	○ AMBER	○ COPPER		○ PALE	○ PALE	○ PALE
○ SALMON	○ PINK	○ RUBY		○ MEDIUM	○ MEDIUM	○ MEDIUM
○ PURPLE	○ GARNET	○ TAWNY		○ DEEP	○ DEEP	○ DEEP

AROMA				TASTE		
○ FRUIT	○ FLORAL	○ HERBAL		○ CITRUS	○ BERRIES	○ COFFEE
○ YEAST	○ SPICE	○ NUT		○ MINERAL	○ SPICE	○ NUT
○ EARTH	○ OAK	○ VEGETAL		○ EARTH	○ BARREL	○ VANILLA
○	○	○		○ COCOA	○	○

SWEETNESS	ACIDITY	TANNINS
1 2 3 4 5 6 7 8 9 10	1 2 3 4 5 6 7 8 9 10	1 2 3 4 5 6 7 8 9 10

BODY	FLAVOR INTENSITY	FINISH
1 2 3 4 5 6 7 8 9 10	1 2 3 4 5 6 7 8 9 10	1 2 3 4 5 6 7 8 9 10

PAIRS WELL WITH	REVIEW NOTES

WOULD YOU BUY IT AGAIN?		OVERALL RATING
○ YES	○ NO	/10

WINE TASTING

NAME		ORCHARD	
ORIGIN		REGION	
TYPE		VARIETAL	
VINTAGE		ALCOHOL %	

HUES

○ STRAW	○ YELLOW	○ GOLD
○ BROWN	○ AMBER	○ COPPER
○ SALMON	○ PINK	○ RUBY
○ PURPLE	○ GARNET	○ TAWNY

INTENSITY

RED	ROSÉ	WHITE
○ PALE	○ PALE	○ PALE
○ MEDIUM	○ MEDIUM	○ MEDIUM
○ DEEP	○ DEEP	○ DEEP

AROMA

○ FRUIT	○ FLORAL	○ HERBAL
○ YEAST	○ SPICE	○ NUT
○ EARTH	○ OAK	○ VEGETAL
○	○	○

TASTE

○ CITRUS	○ BERRIES	○ COFFEE
○ MINERAL	○ SPICE	○ NUT
○ EARTH	○ BARREL	○ VANILLA
○ COCOA	○	○

SWEETNESS	ACIDITY	TANNINS
1 2 3 4 5 6 7 8 9 10	1 2 3 4 5 6 7 8 9 10	1 2 3 4 5 6 7 8 9 10

BODY	FLAVOR INTENSITY	FINISH
1 2 3 4 5 6 7 8 9 10	1 2 3 4 5 6 7 8 9 10	1 2 3 4 5 6 7 8 9 10

PAIRS WELL WITH	REVIEW NOTES

WOULD YOU BUY IT AGAIN?		OVERALL RATING
○ YES	○ NO	/10

WINE TASTING

NAME		ORCHARD	
ORIGIN		REGION	
TYPE		VARIETAL	
VINTAGE		ALCOHOL %	

HUES

○ STRAW	○ YELLOW	○ GOLD
○ BROWN	○ AMBER	○ COPPER
○ SALMON	○ PINK	○ RUBY
○ PURPLE	○ GARNET	○ TAWNY

INTENSITY

RED	ROSÉ	WHITE
○ PALE	○ PALE	○ PALE
○ MEDIUM	○ MEDIUM	○ MEDIUM
○ DEEP	○ DEEP	○ DEEP

AROMA

○ FRUIT	○ FLORAL	○ HERBAL
○ YEAST	○ SPICE	○ NUT
○ EARTH	○ OAK	○ VEGETAL
○	○	○

TASTE

○ CITRUS	○ BERRIES	○ COFFEE
○ MINERAL	○ SPICE	○ NUT
○ EARTH	○ BARREL	○ VANILLA
○ COCOA	○	○

SWEETNESS	ACIDITY	TANNINS
1 2 3 4 5 6 7 8 9 10	1 2 3 4 5 6 7 8 9 10	1 2 3 4 5 6 7 8 9 10

BODY	FLAVOR INTENSITY	FINISH
1 2 3 4 5 6 7 8 9 10	1 2 3 4 5 6 7 8 9 10	1 2 3 4 5 6 7 8 9 10

PAIRS WELL WITH	REVIEW NOTES

WOULD YOU BUY IT AGAIN?		OVERALL RATING
○ YES	○ NO	/10

WINE TASTING

NAME		ORCHARD	
ORIGIN		REGION	
TYPE		VARIETAL	
VINTAGE		ALCOHOL %	

HUES			INTENSITY		
			RED	ROSÉ	WHITE
○ STRAW	○ YELLOW	○ GOLD			
○ BROWN	○ AMBER	○ COPPER	○ PALE	○ PALE	○ PALE
○ SALMON	○ PINK	○ RUBY	○ MEDIUM	○ MEDIUM	○ MEDIUM
○ PURPLE	○ GARNET	○ TAWNY	○ DEEP	○ DEEP	○ DEEP

AROMA			TASTE		
○ FRUIT	○ FLORAL	○ HERBAL	○ CITRUS	○ BERRIES	○ COFFEE
○ YEAST	○ SPICE	○ NUT	○ MINERAL	○ SPICE	○ NUT
○ EARTH	○ OAK	○ VEGETAL	○ EARTH	○ BARREL	○ VANILLA
○	○	○	○ COCOA	○	○

SWEETNESS	ACIDITY	TANNINS
1 2 3 4 5 6 7 8 9 10	1 2 3 4 5 6 7 8 9 10	1 2 3 4 5 6 7 8 9 10

BODY	FLAVOR INTENSITY	FINISH
1 2 3 4 5 6 7 8 9 10	1 2 3 4 5 6 7 8 9 10	1 2 3 4 5 6 7 8 9 10

PAIRS WELL WITH	REVIEW NOTES

WOULD YOU BUY IT AGAIN?		OVERALL RATING
○ YES	○ NO	/10

WINE TASTING

NAME		ORCHARD	
ORIGIN		REGION	
TYPE		VARIETAL	
VINTAGE		ALCOHOL %	

HUES		
○ STRAW	○ YELLOW	○ GOLD
○ BROWN	○ AMBER	○ COPPER
○ SALMON	○ PINK	○ RUBY
○ PURPLE	○ GARNET	○ TAWNY

INTENSITY		
RED	ROSÉ	WHITE
○ PALE	○ PALE	○ PALE
○ MEDIUM	○ MEDIUM	○ MEDIUM
○ DEEP	○ DEEP	○ DEEP

AROMA		
○ FRUIT	○ FLORAL	○ HERBAL
○ YEAST	○ SPICE	○ NUT
○ EARTH	○ OAK	○ VEGETAL
○	○	○

TASTE		
○ CITRUS	○ BERRIES	○ COFFEE
○ MINERAL	○ SPICE	○ NUT
○ EARTH	○ BARREL	○ VANILLA
○ COCOA	○	○

SWEETNESS	ACIDITY	TANNINS
1 2 3 4 5 6 7 8 9 10	1 2 3 4 5 6 7 8 9 10	1 2 3 4 5 6 7 8 9 10

BODY	FLAVOR INTENSITY	FINISH
1 2 3 4 5 6 7 8 9 10	1 2 3 4 5 6 7 8 9 10	1 2 3 4 5 6 7 8 9 10

PAIRS WELL WITH	REVIEW NOTES

WOULD YOU BUY IT AGAIN?		OVERALL RATING
○ YES	○ NO	/10

WINE TASTING

NAME		ORCHARD	
ORIGIN		REGION	
TYPE		VARIETAL	
VINTAGE		ALCOHOL %	

HUES			INTENSITY		
			RED	ROSÉ	WHITE
○ STRAW	○ YELLOW	○ GOLD			
○ BROWN	○ AMBER	○ COPPER	○ PALE	○ PALE	○ PALE
○ SALMON	○ PINK	○ RUBY	○ MEDIUM	○ MEDIUM	○ MEDIUM
○ PURPLE	○ GARNET	○ TAWNY	○ DEEP	○ DEEP	○ DEEP

AROMA			TASTE		
○ FRUIT	○ FLORAL	○ HERBAL	○ CITRUS	○ BERRIES	○ COFFEE
○ YEAST	○ SPICE	○ NUT	○ MINERAL	○ SPICE	○ NUT
○ EARTH	○ OAK	○ VEGETAL	○ EARTH	○ BARREL	○ VANILLA
○	○	○	○ COCOA	○	○

SWEETNESS	ACIDITY	TANNINS
1 2 3 4 5 6 7 8 9 10	1 2 3 4 5 6 7 8 9 10	1 2 3 4 5 6 7 8 9 10

BODY	FLAVOR INTENSITY	FINISH
1 2 3 4 5 6 7 8 9 10	1 2 3 4 5 6 7 8 9 10	1 2 3 4 5 6 7 8 9 10

PAIRS WELL WITH	REVIEW NOTES

WOULD YOU BUY IT AGAIN?		OVERALL RATING
○ YES	○ NO	/10

www.ingramcontent.com/pod-product-compliance
Lightning Source LLC
Chambersburg PA
CBHW071421070526
44578CB00003B/650